Un-Complicating the Constitution

BY CHAD KENT

Un-Complicating the Constitution
© 2013 by Chad Kent

Published by Chad Kent Speaks, LLC
Frisco, TX

ISBN: 978-0-615-91133-5

Acknowledgements

To start, I need to thank my Lord and Savior Jesus Christ who has blessed me more than I could ever deserve. He is the one who ultimately gave me the strength and talents necessary to write this book and it is through him that all things are possible.

I want to give a sincere and heart-felt thank you to everyone who helped and supported me while I was writing this book. First and most importantly to my wife, Sarah, who did far more than her share of house work during this process to make sure I had time to write. She also spent many nights as a sounding board for ideas and as an editor who has read this entire book 10 times at least. From day one she has believed in me and been by far my strongest supporter.

I would like to thank Bailey Connell, Melissa Denker, Amy Noland and everyone who read sample chapters and endured me badgering them about feedback. Your thoughts were more helpful than you can imagine. Gary Kilpatrick also deserves a very special thank you. He volunteered to go through this book line by line to edit for both content and typos. Gary was also a great source of encouragement as well.

Thank you to Darren LaCroix for setting such a great example of how to behave as a professional and for being an unwavering supporter. Your belief in me gave me the confidence to always keep moving forward no matter what happened.

Finally, I want to send a gigantic thank you to Sylvia Acuff who grabbed on to this project and pushed it across the finish line. If it weren't for her organizing all of the details of getting this book ready to be published it would probably never would have gotten done.

"This book presents the Constitution in an understandable way and emphasizes how current it still is today. The schools have failed in recent years to educate our youth about our founding principles that have carried us to the top, while those of us who are older need to be reminded. This book is a must for every American citizen, or one aspiring to become one."

— Del Harris

M.A. American history, Former Coach of LA Lakers and NBA Coach of the Year, ordained minister, and author of "On Point - Four Steps to Better Life Teams"

Introduction

"THE END OF LAW IS, NOT TO ABOLISH OR RESTRAIN, BUT TO PRESERVE AND ENLARGE FREEDOM."
— John Locke[1]

As Americans, we have been blessed to live in the greatest nation in history. This country has offered us a level of freedom that most people in the world today couldn't even imagine. But in recent decades, we have seen the United States steadily declining and our freedom quickly being eroded.

So how did we go from a nation that was founded on the idea that the primary role of government is to protect our rights to one that lays down rules that restrict every area of our lives?

There are a lot of factors that have gotten us to this point, but they all lead back to the same core problem. Over the last 100 years, we have allowed academics, lawyers, and politicians (who I will refer to throughout this book as "the experts") to tell us what the Constitution means. We no longer take responsibility as citizens for learning the Constitution ourselves so that we are prepared to protect our freedom.

> "We are under a Constitution, but the Constitution is what the judges say it is."
> — Charles Evans Hughes

This quote from former Chief Justice of the Supreme Court Charles Evans Hughes perfectly illustrates the problem. What he's saying here is, "Sure, we have a Constitution but regular folks like you don't need to worry about that. The Constitution means what experts tell you it means."

Does that sound like an attitude that will lead our country to freedom?

Does this sound like the statement of a public servant or a ruler?

From his speech in Elmira, New York May 3, 1907
The Autobiographical Notes of Charles Evans Hughes

[1] From The Second Treatise of Government

Here's a great example of that. Last year I was working on a project with some people who worked as staff members for our representatives in Congress. During the course of conversation, I asked one of them, "So does the Constitution even matter when you're writing bills?"

"Oh yeah," he told me. "It's really important. We send them all right over to the Congressional Research Service and they tell us exactly what's Constitutional."

What this Congressional staffer made clear during our conversation was that he wasn't at all interested in judging the Constitutionality of these bills himself. He wasn't worried about whether they were consistent with the principles of good government or if they would protect our freedom. His primary concern was figuring out what the experts over at the Supreme Court would let Congress get away with.

My Congressional staffer friend - like so many Americans today - was perfectly content to sit back and let others tell him what the Constitution means. By doing that, he was giving other people the power to tell him exactly how much freedom he should be allowed to have.

It's time for all of that to stop. If we want to have any chance at remaining a free people, then we as citizens must take the Constitution back from the experts.

Throughout our lives we've been told that the Constitution is far too complicated for regular people to understand so we need to leave it to the experts. That is a complete and total lie. Our Constitution is actually quite simple. In fact, it has to be. Here's why.

> **"Laws are made for men of ordinary understanding, and should therefore be construed by the ordinary rules of common sense."**
>
> — Thomas Jefferson
>
> Letter to Justice William Johnson
> June 12, 1823

The United States was designed to be a self-government; a nation where the average person was able to govern himself. In that case, our Constitution had to be simple enough for the average farmer, baker, or merchant to understand. If only an "expert" could understand the Constitution, that alone would destroy the idea of self-government.

But in order to continue that tradition of self-government, the regular citizens of today - like you and me - need to make sure that we understand our Constitution and how it was intended to work. Fortunately, the Constitution and the ideas of our Founders are very accessible. Don't get me wrong - they are extraordinarily brilliant. But they are easy to understand.

You might be thinking, "What do you mean the Constitution is simple?! Every time I hear people on tv talking about legal issues or Supreme

Court cases it's so complicated I end up with a headache." And you're right, the way they discuss Constitutional law on television is confusing (and usually frustrating). But those discussions have little if anything to do with the ideas of our Founders.

Over the last 100 years our modern experts have made dramatic changes to how the Constitution is applied in this country. It's this new way of applying the Constitution that the tv pundits are talking about.

The main reason that our modern approach is so much more confusing is the fact that the experts no longer look at freedom or protecting the rights of individuals as the ultimate goal. Their ideas for government are usually aimed at creating social justice, diversity, or some other perceived social good.

When you become more concerned with protecting fairness and creating equal outcomes than you are with protecting individual rights and creating freedom, it requires a confusing labyrinth of laws. You'll need laws to keep some people from getting too far ahead and laws to make sure others aren't falling too far behind. You'll need laws to make sure there are enough women in some jobs and laws to make sure there are enough men in other jobs, and on and on it goes. It's that confusing labyrinth of laws that you hear being discussed on television - and as you may have noticed - it has very little to do with the Constitution.

You also may have noticed that the new approach to government isn't working very well. Our country is trillions of dollars in debt, our rights are being trampled on from all directions, and our ability to pursue our dreams is being severely limited by government interference.

This book will help you see exactly why this new approach isn't working. As we move through the following chapters, we are going to discuss six of the principles of good government that our Constitution was built on. Once you understand these principles, it will not only make it easier for you to learn the specifics of the Constitution, you will be much better prepared to defend your freedom.

Need Proof?

Lest you doubt my assertion that the experts think they are the only ones who should be interpreting the Constitution, try a fun little experiment for me. Actually, this one is worth doing just for the entertainment value.

Go up to a lawyer or a college professor and tell them you want to explain how you think a certain clause of the Constitution should be interpreted. Nine out of ten times, the condescension you get in return will be extraordinary.

DEFINING FREEDOM

If you asked most Americans what the purpose of our government is, you'd probably hear the word "freedom" somewhere in just about every answer. That's what most of us sincerely want. But if freedom is our goal, we need to be clear about what that means. Until we define what true freedom is, we won't ever be able to design a strategy for making it a reality. That's just common sense. You wouldn't start cooking your dinner without first defining what it is you intend to make, would you? Of course not. If you just started haphazardly throwing ingredients into a bowl and cooked them in a completely random way, you have virtually no chance of ending up with something edible.

Each time you start preparing your dinner, you start by defining exactly what you plan to make and how many people you will be feeding. Once you've figured out what your goal is, then you can start taking the steps necessary to get there.

The same thing is true with government. We need to decide what our goal is before we haphazardly start creating policies. So before I get into the principles that create freedom, I'm going to start by defining exactly what freedom is and what it isn't.

> "[Tyrannical governments] cover the surface of society with a network of small complicated rules, minute and uniform, through which the most original minds and the most energetic characters cannot penetrate to rise above the crowd. The will of man is not shattered but softened, bent and guided; men are seldom forced by it to act, but they are constantly restrained from acting. Such a power does not destroy, but it prevents existence; it does not tyrannize, but it compresses, enervates, extinguishes, and stupefies people, till each nation is reduced to being nothing more than a flock of timid industrial animals, of which the government is the shepherd."
>
> — Alexis de Tocqueville
> Democracy in America

An endless list of small, complicated rules for everything we do. Does that sound like our country today? If you aren't sure about the answer to that, think about how complicated it is just to pay your taxes!! Heck, I hire someone to do it for me because I can't even begin to understand all the rules.

As Hayek explains here, when a government creates that kind of minefield of rules for you to follow it keeps you from reaching your potential in life. Granted, our government might not be actively destroying us as we've seen happen in other countries throughout history but we need to realize that it is preventing us from truly living.

WHAT IS FREEDOM?

Freedom means having the greatest amount of control over the direction of your own life as you possibly can. It means being able to pursue happiness in your life without the government getting in your way. As Bastiat[2] explains in the quote to the right, freedom is being able to make whatever you want out of your life as long as you don't violate someone else's rights in the process of doing so.

Freedom is a very simple concept and one that has been extremely powerful in enabling people to live fulfilling and prosperous lives.

But for years the experts have been trying to confuse you about the meaning of that word. They will tell you that "true" freedom means freedom from worry and freedom from want.[3] Their argument is that it isn't possible for a person to exercise his freedom if he doesn't have the tools necessary - like food, shelter, or an education.

> **In short, is not liberty the freedom of every person to make full use of his faculties, so long as he does not harm other persons while doing so?**
>
> — Frederic Bastiat
> The Law

The main solution the experts give us for this problem is to have the government take property away from some people in society and give that property to someone else who is less fortunate. But in that situation no one has freedom. Not the person who is having his money taken from him and given to someone else (a violation of his right to property) - and certainly not the person who now has to depend on government for his survival.

Freedom cannot involve dependence - those two words are polar opposites. Let's look at why.

"DEPENDENCE IS VERY LITTLE ELSE BUT AN OBLIGATION TO CONFORM TO THE WILL OR LAW OF THAT SUPERIOR PERSON OR STATE UPON WHICH THE INFERIOR DEPENDS."

— William Blackstone
Commentaries on the Laws of England

---

[2] Frederic Bastiat was a French economist and politician who lived from 1801 - 1850.

[3] Perhaps the best example of this comes from Franklin Delano Roosevelt. In 1944 he proposed a "Second Bill of Rights" that would guarantee everyone a "right" to housing, education, and health care. To justify this he said, "We have come to a clear realization of the fact that true individual freedom cannot exist without economic security and independence."

As long as the government provides for you, it owns you. When you were growing up, did you ever hear the phrase, "As long as you live under my roof, you'll live under my rules?" That isn't just true with parents, it's also true with the government.

Imagine that you rely on the government for food stamps. Since the government is providing you food, it can also tell you what you can eat, how much, and at what time or place. If you don't want to submit to those rules, it can take your food away.

You might think I'm taking this theory too far and that the government would never do any of that in real life. But if you think politicians wouldn't use welfare as an excuse to tell you what to eat, I have news for you: It already does. Have you ever seen one of these at the grocery store:

This sign is the government saying that this particular food has been approved to be purchased by food stamps. If you legitimately need those food stamps, then you will be forced to eat what the government tells you that you can eat.

In this situation where you are told what you can eat and how much, how free are you really?

The obvious answer is: you're not. You are at the mercy of our politicians. As long as you live under the government's roof, you have to live the way it tells you to.

When we create a environment where we are dependent on government, we give control of our lives over to politicians. No longer are we free to live our lives how we choose. Instead, we are forced to conform to rules that are made for us in Washington D.C. as a requirement of getting the benefits we need to survive.

That is not freedom. At its most basic level, freedom is having the liberty to make your own choices in life. The more choices you are able to make in life without government interference, the more free you are.

WHAT'S SO GREAT ABOUT BEING FREE?

There is a reason why people risk their lives to try to come to the United States from all over the world: they know that once they are free, *anything is possible*. When they are free they can make their lives whatever they want them to be.

What could be more fulfilling than having control over your own life? To live your life according to your conscience? To be your own man or woman? It is the single greatest blessing that God can grant us in this life.

Being able to decide what direction you want your life to take allows you to dream big dreams, then go out and see if you've got what it takes to make them a reality. Just knowing that anything is possible is what inspires ordinary people to do extraordinary things.

When we are allowed to be free it unleashes a spirit and a determination that cannot be found any other way. That spirit of freedom is perfectly illustrated in the following quote[4]:

I do not choose to be a common man.

It is my right to be uncommon—if I can.

I seek opportunity—not security. I do not wish to be a kept citizen, humbled and dulled by having the state look after me.

I want to take the calculated risk; to dream and to build, to fail and to succeed.

I refuse to barter incentive for a dole. I prefer the challenges of life to the guaranteed existence; the thrill of fulfillment to the stale calm of utopia.

I will not trade freedom for beneficence nor my dignity for a handout. I will never cower before any master nor bend to any threat.

It is my heritage to stand erect, proud and unafraid; to think and act for myself, enjoy the benefit of my creations and to face the world boldly and say, "This I have done."

To think for yourself, to act for yourself, and to keep what you've created. Now that is freedom!

---

[4] This quote is often attributed to Teddy Roosevelt but I can find no evidence of that. Regardless of who made this comment, it nails the attitude of a free man.

I hesitated to include this quote because of its connection to Teddy Roosevelt. He was not a friend to our Constitution by any stretch and we will discuss one example of why in Chapter 2. It's unfortunate that he didn't reflect the attitude of this quote in many of his actions and comments as president.

The person who said this chooses to be uncommon. He clearly chooses to experience all that life has to offer and reach his greatest potential in life. What do you choose to do? Maybe for you the perfect life is to dedicate yourself to being the best parent you can be. Maybe you want to give back to your community and start a charitable organization. Maybe you don't even care what you do for a living as long as you earn enough money to pay for the hobbies you love on the weekend. It really doesn't matter... the point is that **you** get to decide.

What could be more fun or more fulfilling than that?!

OK, FREEDOM ROCKS. SO HOW DO WE MAKE IT A REALITY?

Government is just like anything else in life - it's a cause and effect game. If freedom is the effect that we want, then we need to learn what principles cause freedom and implement them. To put it even more simply, we need to figure out what causes people to be free... and then go do that.

But we have to make a conscious decision to create freedom because it doesn't happen by accident. Governments don't naturally embrace freedom for individuals.

For a moment, let's go back to the example of you cooking your dinner. A tasty meal doesn't happen by accident. If you put a bunch of different ingredients together and give absolutely no consideration to what they are, you aren't going to end up with anything you want to eat.

The same is true with government. Before we can create and protect freedom for individuals, we need to have a strategy. If we just haphazardly throw a bunch of policies together without carefully considering how they work together, we aren't going to end up with the type of country we want to live in. We'll be left with the type of government that does happen by accident - **tyranny**[5].

The great part is, we don't have to settle for that. We can take our Constitution back from the experts and ensure that we continue to enjoy the fulfillment of being able to control the direction of our own lives. The first step to doing that is learning the six principles that a government must follow to preserve freedom. This book will help you understand each of those principles and how they apply to our world today. So let's get started by learning about the first principle - all men are created equal.

---

[5] Dictionary.com defines tyranny as "oppressive or unjustly severe government on the part of any ruler." If you want to understand what people are trying to get across when they use this word, just picture an out of control government that is trying to run every detail of your life.

We say all men are created equal... shouldn't we act like it?

Principle 1: All men are created equal

Imagine that you're designing a new airplane. How important would it be for you to understand and follow the laws of physics and aerodynamics? Pretty darned important, right? If your design violates the laws of physics then your plane is never going to get off the ground.

You may not like certain aspects of the laws of physics but there's absolutely nothing you can do to change them. Sure, you can ignore the laws that are inconvenient - like gravity in this case - or you can try to come up with new ones that you think are better. But if that's the case, well... let's just say I wouldn't want to be your test pilot.

The same is true when you're designing a government. There are certain laws that govern the way that human beings behave and the way they interact with each other. Before you can create a government that will be successful, you have to understand these aspects of Natural Law.

Natural Law - or what Thomas Jefferson described in the Declaration of Independence as the "Laws of nature and of nature's God" - is basically the way God created the world to work. What goes up must come down. The sun rises in the east. All of those basic facts of life. If we intend to be successful in anything we do, we need to make sure we are following Natural Law.

Any government that is going to be effective in protecting our liberty must be designed and administered in a way that is consistent with Natural Law.

Even though some of those Natural Laws might be frustrating or inconvenient, we can't change them. Frankly, I hate the fact that the days get a lot shorter in the winter. I could try to petition members of Congress to fix that for me and I might even be able to convince them to pass a law mandating the sun to stay out for an extra three hours in the winter. But in the end, we'd all be disappointed because the sun has a tendency to ignore man-made laws.

And in this silly example lies the single greatest key to creating a government that will secure and protect individual freedom - the laws of nature are superior to any manmade law. We cannot change that under any circumstance so if we want our government to be effective it has to be designed in a way that is consistent with Natural Law.

Any time that we try to enact a policy through our government that violates Natural Law, that policy will always fail. Every time. The principles that you are going to explore throughout this book were critical to designing our Constitution and every one of them flows directly from Natural Law.

Perhaps the most fundamental law of nature when it comes to government is the principle that all men are created equal. In today's world, human equality is just a matter of common sense for most of us. But despite that, it's important to take a look at the reasons why it's true because the background will help you get a better understanding of some of the principles that will come later in this book.

Let's say you were to walk into a nursery and you saw two newborns laying side by side. Would you be able to tell which of the two babies was superior and naturally prepared to rule over the other? Of course not - that would be impossible.

Thomas Jefferson perfectly illustrated why that is when he said:

"The general spread of the light of science has already laid open to every view the palpable truth, that the mass of mankind has not been born with saddles on their backs, nor a favored few booted and spurred, ready to ride them legitimately, by the grace of god."[1]

If there were a small number of people who were inherently superior to the rest of us and intended to rule over society, there would be a distinct characteristic that would allow us to identify them. The fact that there isn't should tell us that there is no "naturally chosen ruling class". We are all created equal.

However, the fact that all men are created equal doesn't mean that we are all born with equal *abilities*. Lord knows that all you have to do to prove that is watch me compete with my wife in virtually anything. I still remember the first time we went bowling together. Being a typical guy, I envisioned a night where I would show her how to play and then take it easy on her to make sure I didn't beat her too badly. Then she went out and bowled a 209. I don't know how she does it! The two of us are a perfect illustration of the fact that we were all created with unique talents and some people will achieve more in life than others. That's just the way the world works.

Human equality means that we all have equal *value* and we all have an equal claim to our rights. If the richest most powerful man in the country has his rights violated, it should be treated no differently under the law than if the poorest, most irrelevant man has his rights violated. It is a

[1] Thomas Jefferson, Letter to Roger C. Weightman, June 24, 1826

tragedy in both cases. We are all equal in the eyes of God, and because of that, we must all be equal in the eyes of the government.

HOW DO THE EXPERTS VIOLATE THIS CONCEPT?

Because of our equal value, there is never a justification for violating one person's rights for the purpose of benefiting another person. Unfortunately, our politicians are constantly creating policies that do exactly that. The one that you are probably most familiar with is our progressive income tax.

A progressive income tax - like the one we have in the United States - is one where you pay a higher rate if you earn a higher income. The more money you make, the greater percentage the government is going to take in taxes. Under this system not all citizens stand equally before the law. A person who has a lot of money will be held to a much different set of laws than a person with very little money.

You've probably heard the arguments behind this kind of tax. We have to make sure that the rich pay their "fair share" so that the government can afford expensive entitlement programs. In other words, we should take more money away from wealthy people for the benefit of those who aren't as well off. But is that consistent with the idea that all men are created equal?

Absolutely not. John Adams explained why:

"It is agreed 'that the end of all government is the good
and ease of the people in a secure enjoyment of their rights,
without oppression'; but it must be remembered, that the rich
are people as well as the poor; that they have rights as well as
others; that they have as clear and as sacred a right to their large
property as others have to theirs which is smaller; that oppression
to them is as possible and as wicked as to others."[2]

What Adams is saying here, is that government was created to protect the rights of everyone in the country. The fact that someone is wealthy doesn't make it ok for us to treat him differently. Violating a person's rights is always a tragedy regardless of who he is.

Believe it or not, rich people are, in fact, people. It's shocking, I know. As Adams points out, rich people have property rights just like the rest of us and the fact that they have a lot of property doesn't change that. But under a progressive income tax, when a person becomes wealthier and wealthier the government treats him as if he has less and less of a right to keep his property.

Let's use two fictional people to illustrate that. Jerry earns $50,000

[2] John Adams, Defence of the Constitutions of Government of the United States of America.

per year and falls into the 10% tax bracket. Tommy earns $200,000 and falls into the 30% bracket. In this scenario, every time Jerry goes out and earns another $1 the government says it has a right to take 10 cents of it. But every time Tommy works to earn one more $1 the government says it has a right to take 30 cents from him. So under this tax system, Tommy has less of a right to keep the fruits of his labor.

You might say, "So what? Tommy can afford to pay a little more; look how much money he makes." It doesn't matter. Remember, any time we enact a policy that violates the principle that all men are created equal, that policy is destined to fail. We are already seeing the negative effects of this progressive tax system in this country.

Progressive taxation has played a major role in the political division we see in the country today and made it easier for our politicians to create our current financial mess as well. Since the government no longer has to treat everyone as if they are equal - and have an equal right to the property they earn - the politicians can pit different groups of Americans against each other.

In the middle of campaign season a politician can go up to Jerry and say, "If you vote for me, I'll raise Tommy's taxes so that I can pay for some great government programs that will benefit you." That's a dangerous situation to create because it allows Jerry to support a higher spending, bigger government while feeling like he isn't going to have to bear any of the burden of paying for it. You may have noticed that it also gives politicians an easy way to buy votes.

Over the years, our politicians have taken this approach a step further. The conversation has now turned into, "Look at that Tommy. Isn't he evil? It's not fair that he has so much money. We should raise his taxes. We need to make sure he pays his fair share." So progressive taxation has actually made it possible for politicians and political parties to benefit from pitting Americans against each other.

There are always consequences to violating Natural Law. In this case, violating the principle that all men are created equal has made it much easier for our government to spend money recklessly and divide us as a nation. That division - combined with the huge debt we've created - may end up being what destroys this country.

How different do you think the result would be if our politician in the example above had to go to Jerry and say, "I've got this new idea for a great program, but it's going to require me to raise your taxes..."? Most likely Jerry is going to put a lot more thought into how much he really wants that new program because he knows he's going to have to pay for part of it. He no longer has the option of picking Tommy's pocket to get what he wants.

But as things stand today, we basically have half of the people in this country voting to decide how much money they will take from the other half and what to spend it on. That's not a recipe for sound policy or fiscal discipline.

Unfortunately, this is far from the only way that we violate the fact that all men are created equal. The way our government operates today, passing laws that do treat all citizens equally is the exception rather than the rule. It's rare to see a bill passed that doesn't contain some special loophole to make sure it doesn't apply to politically favored businesses or groups of people.

In other words, our politicians love to talk about their commitment to equality, but they don't put those words into action. Do you think their complete disregard for Natural Law (ie. how the world was designed to work) might explain why our country is now facing so many major problems?

HOW DOES THIS SHOW UP IN THE CONSTITUTION?

The principle that all men are created equal can be seen throughout the Constitution in a variety of ways. For example:

- The rights that are protected in the Bill of Rights are unconditional. There is no mention of them only applying to property owners or men, etc. Everyone has these rights.
- As the Constitution was originally written, taxes had to be applied uniformly throughout the country. In other words, they had to be applied to everyone, in every area of the country, in exactly the same way. Sadly, that was changed by the 16th Amendment.[3]

Both of these aspects of the Constitution required the government to treat everyone as if they were equal.

However, when it comes to this particular principle, probably the best way to demonstrate Natural Law is to discuss where it *doesn't* show up

[3] There are two sections of the Constitution that discuss uniform taxation.

The first one is Article 1, Section 8 where it says that "all Duties, Imposts, and Excises shall be uniform throughout the United States."

The second one is in Article 1, Section 9 where it says that Congress can only lay taxes directly on the people if those taxes are proportionate to the population of the states. What that means is, if you take the total amount collected by this direct tax in each state and divide it by that state's population, the average amount per person had to be the same in every state. It's really confusing, I know. But the idea here is make sure that Congress could not impose a tax that would require the citizens in one state or a few states to carry a heavier burden than the citizens in others.

The 16th Amendment changed that and granted Congress the authority to tax your income directly without having to worry about keeping the tax burden proportionate among the states. That paved the way for the progressive income tax we talked about earlier in this chapter.

On a side note, the 16th Amendment was ratified in 1913 - before that there was no income tax. How great would life be if you didn't have to worry about doing the chore of figuring out your taxes and sending them in every April 15th?

in the Constitution. It's the elephant in the room that you were probably asking yourself about as you read the last paragraph - slavery.

Our Founders were brilliant men with a great understanding of Natural Law - but this is the one major area where they didn't insist on following it in the Constitution. There is certainly a lot of debate about that decision. Should those Founders who knew slavery was evil have demanded that it be abolished even if that meant the southern states would leave the country? Or was it prudent to make some compromises in hopes that they could have enough influence over the southern states to abolish slavery there too?

For our purposes, the bottom line is that the principle that all men are created equal was not upheld in the earliest years of this nation. The fact that slavery was allowed to exist was a **huge** violation of Natural Law. As you know, there are always consequences to violating Natural Law and this case was no different. We had to pay a massive price for allowing slavery to continue.

We paid that price in three ways. First, millions of innocent men and women had their rights violated and their lives destroyed. It's a tragedy any time that one person's rights are violated - let alone millions of people over a period of decades.

Second, we will never know what great works the world will never see because of the way we oppressed those people. Had we allowed them to be educated and live in freedom, who knows what great works of art or literature they may have created, what inventions they could have designed, or the great humanitarian work they could have done. We will never know how much the world has lost because of that decision to allow slavery to continue.

Finally, 600,000 Americans gave their lives during the Civil War - the bloodiest war in our nation's history.

All of these consequences were a direct result of our decision not to treat all men as equals. You would think after an experience like that we'd learn our lesson about how important it is to understand and follow Natural Law. But we haven't.

We are still implementing policies that act as if all men aren't created equal. For example, we have affirmative action policies that judge people differently based on race or gender and abortion laws that treat a person who is in the womb as if he has no rights at all. You may like and support those policies but the fact is that they violate Natural Law, so they are all destined to have negative effects on our society. That's just the way the world works.

It's unfortunate that the concept of "equality" has become something of a cliche over the years and now we take it for granted without even thinking about it. If we want to continue to enjoy the blessings of freedom, the concept that all men are created equal has to be more than a cute slogan or an empty platitude. It must be a guiding principle that influences our thoughts and actions - even when that requires us to make tough decisions.

If we are serious about our belief in human equality, then logically we also have to come to a few other conclusions about human nature and how a government should operate. Each chapter in this book will explore a separate conclusion that flows directly from this first Natural Law principle that all men are created equal. As you'll see by the time you finish, in a world where all men are created equal, a constitutionally limited, representative government is the only morally justifiable system of government possible.

Without rights, what's left?

Principle 2: We are all created with equal rights

"I AM AWARE OF ONLY TWO MEANS OF ESTABLISHING EQUALITY IN THE WORLD OF POLITICS: RIGHTS HAVE TO BE GRANTED TO EVERY CITIZEN OR TO NONE."

— Alexis de Tocqueville
Democracy in America

Y ou don't have to work very hard in today's world to hear people talking about rights. Worker's rights, gay rights, women's rights, animal rights, puppet rights - these discussions are everywhere. But what are rights? And why are they so important?

In a lot of ways, your rights are like your home. Your home is your personal space that you own and that *no one* has a right to enter without your permission - not even the government. In the same way, your rights are the areas of your life where you as an individual have absolute authority. No one has the authority to violate those areas of your life without your permission.

To illustrate that, think about an obvious right like the Freedom of Religion. You and you alone can choose what you truly believe and how you choose to worship God. No other person or government on earth has any legitimate authority to force you to do otherwise.

These areas of your life are so sacred that they cannot be violated without also violating you as a person - without violating your humanity. Our rights are a part of what makes us human and separates us from the animals. They are a part of us the moment we are created.

"Is there a limit to how we can use our rights?"

Yes, just one. You never have a right to do something that violates the rights of another person. The simplest and most common way to explain that is the fact that I have a right to swing my fists around all I want. However, my right to swing my fist ends where your nose begins. So my rights end where your rights begin, and vice versa.

As you know from the last chapter, we were all created equal. So naturally we all have equal rights. There can be no special women's rights or worker's rights - there are only individual rights that we *all* have as human beings. The idea that women, racial groups, workers, etc. might have special rights is incompatible with the fact that all men are created equal. If different groups of people each have unique sets of rights, they cannot be equal.

THREE BASIC CATEGORIES OF RIGHTS

Anything that can properly be called a right will fit into one of three categories: the right to life, the right to liberty, and the right to property. Let's look at where each one of these categories of rights comes from logically.

Right to Life

If all men are created equal, then who could possibly own you but you? Obviously, if we are all equal then it's not possible for someone else to be born with a natural claim to run your life for you. It only stands to reason that you own yourself and your body.

Your life is your own and you alone get to choose what to do with it. No one else has any authority to take your life from you or harm you physically in any way. To put this another way, if we are all equal, what justification could one person have for deciding if someone else should live or die? None whatsoever.

Clearly you have an inherent, God-given right to life.

Right to Liberty

If you own yourself, who should be able to tell you what you can do with yourself or to yourself? *As long as you aren't violating the rights of anyone else*, your right to use your body as you choose is absolute. After all, it's yours.

In a lot of ways your body is similar to your other possessions.. You would never question the fact that you should be able to do whatever you want with your television as long as you don't hurt anyone besides yourself. Again, it's your television. You could throw it off the roof of your house and no one would care.

Because your body is your possession, you can do whatever you want with it as long as you aren't harming anyone else. Clearly, you have an inherent, God-given right to liberty.

Right to Property

If you own yourself and you choose to use yourself to create something of value, who else should own your creation but you? After all, you created it.

To illustrate that, I'll borrow an example that John Locke[1] explains in his *Second Treatise on Government*. Imagine that you are living in nature and there is no government at all. One day, you decide to clear a piece of land and plant some corn there. Once you've done that, you spend the next few months carefully tending to your crop. Not surprisingly, your little plot of land ends up producing a whole lot more corn at the end of the year than it would have if you weren't there.

Where did all that extra corn come from? It's a product of the extra labor that you chose to put into the land. Since the labor belongs to you, the product of your labor belongs to you as well. No other person has any right to what you've produced because - without you - there wouldn't be any property to own in the first place.

Today's world is much more complicated than this but the concept still applies. If you decide to sell your labor to someone else in exchange for money (ie. you get a job), the money you earn is yours. It doesn't matter what you create or how you create it - as long as you don't violate the rights of someone else - that object is your property and you have a right to keep it.

Clearly, you have an inherent, God-given right to property.

OK, SO I HAVE RIGHTS. WHY DOES THAT MATTER?

Understanding exactly what our rights are is critical because they are the area of your life where you as an individual have absolute authority. Our rights are so essential to what makes us human that they cannot be violated without also degrading our humanity. They create a boundary line that no one - including the government - can cross without violating Natural Law.

In fact, natural rights are so important that without them, freedom is impossible. Let me say that again just for emphasis. Unless we, as human beings, have unalienable natural rights, freedom is impossible. The reason for that is simple. If there isn't something unique and sacred about human life, then why shouldn't the government or another person be able to do whatever it wants with you?

---

[1] John Locke was an English political philosopher whose writing had a major impact on the thinking of our Founders. If you read The Second Treatise of Government - his most important work - it is very easy to see the influence it had on our Declaration of Independence.

HOW ARE THE EXPERTS VIOLATING THIS CONCEPT?

As long as we demand that our rights be respected, that limits how much power the government can have. But remember, it's **human nature**[2] for people to like having power and to try to get more and more of it. So people in government are always going to come up with clever ways to convince you that there is some urgent need to violate our rights. If they can do that successfully, it allows them to have more power.

One method that is popular with lawyers and judges now is to use the phrase "compelling government interest." That sounds super-duper legalistic and intellectual doesn't it? Basically it means the government found something that it really wants to do and it doesn't care if it has to violate your natural rights to do it.

> **"Our rights precede human legislation and are therefore superior to it."**
>
> — Frederic Bastiat
> The Law

The Supreme Court laid out its point of view on this pretty clearly in the 1963 case *NAACP v. Button:*

> **"The decisions of this Court have consistently held that only a compelling state interest in the regulation of a subject within the State's constitutional power to regulate can justify limiting First Amendment freedoms."**

So in other words, the government can't violate your rights unless it has a really good reason to (ie. a compelling interest). Doesn't that make you feel safe?

The entire concept is nonsense. The single most compelling interest a government has is to protect the rights of citizens - that is the primary purpose it was created for.[3]

This argument is no different than if a school were to argue that it's going to have to limit the education it offered its students because it had a "com-

---

[2] Human nature is the way people behave instinctively. For example, my wife and I have twin boys. When they got to be about 18 months old, it was pretty common for one to be in our living room playing with a toy when the other one would come up and take the toy away. What would the first boy do? He would turn around and smack his brother for taking the toy away.

Now believe it or not, my wife and I don't hit each other - and we didn't teach our boys to steal - so where did they learn that behavior? They didn't. It's just part of human nature.

Some aspects of human nature that are important to keep in mind when it comes to government are the fact that people are prone to be greedy, they are easily corrupted by power, and they are self-interested (ie. they will take care of themselves first before they take care of others).

[3] Thomas Jefferson explained this in the Declaration of Independence:

"We hold these truths to be self-evident, that all men are created equal, that they are endowed by their Creator with certain unalienable rights, that among these are Life, Liberty, and the pursuit of Happiness.— That to secure these rights, Governments are instituted among Men...

pelling school interest" in providing great lunches. Sure, providing a quality lunch is nice for a school to do, but it was created to educate its students.

Nonetheless, you'll see government lawyers going into court today and arguing that your Freedom of Religion should be restricted because the government has a compelling interest in education. While an argument can be made that local governments have a role to play in educating our children, that's never a justification for violating our rights. Individual rights are the trump card.

While I'm on the topic of a trump card, let's do one last analogy to make sure this part is clear for you - it truly is *that* important.

Imagine you are playing a game of poker and you get dealt a royal flush - the highest hand you could possibly have. Nothing beats a royal flush. Nothing. After playing the hand it finally comes time for everyone to show their cards and you lay down your royal flush. At that point, the guy across from you insists that he should win because his full house is a very compelling hand as well.

Is there any possible way that you'd shrug and say, "You're right. A full house is pretty awesome."? Of course not!

That is why you need to understand the nature of your rights. Your rights are a royal flush. So when our politicians come to you and say, "We're going to have to limit your freedom of speech but we have a really good reason," you can look them in the eye and say, "Too bad, I've got rights. Read 'em and weep."

Protecting your rights is the *most* compelling government interest possible. Nothing takes precedent over that.

HOW CAN YOU TELL WHAT'S A RIGHT AND WHAT ISN'T?

A lot of people today are under the impression that a "right" is anything that they really, really want to do or to have. Pay attention the next few times you hear people discussing politics and you'll notice that this word comes up a lot.

It's common now to hear young people make comments like, "I went to college for four years. I have a right to a high paying job when I graduate." No, actually you don't. A high paying job is something you want, not something you have a right to. No one is under any obligation to hire you.

Having said all that, how the heck can you tell what is a right and what isn't? Well, when you are trying to answer that question there are three basic characteristics that you need to keep in mind:

• Exercising a right must not require the participation of another person
• Exercising a right must not take anything from another person
• Exercising a right must not require the government to grant you that right

Anything that doesn't meet all three criteria simply is not a right. Let's look at each characteristic individually:

Exercising a right must not require the participation of another person:

As you saw earlier in this chapter, rights are a part of Natural Law. They are a part of your humanity that is with you from the moment you are created. Even if you live in a place where there is no government at all, you still have rights. Because of that, a right must be something you can exercise in the absence of government. Anything that would require the government to force someone to do something for you or with you is not a right.

No legitimate right can require you to violate the rights of someone else. If the government forces another person to do something for you, that is by definition a violation of their right to liberty.

For example, it has become very popular now for people to say, "I happen to believe that healthcare is a human right." A lot of folks do that because they believe this claim makes them sound compassionate and intellectual - but it's complete nonsense.

How exactly would a "right" to healthcare work?

Imagine that you're living out in a remote forest where there is no government and you get sick. One day, as you are out walking you miraculously manage to run into a doctor who can treat you. How exactly do you get him to fulfill your "right" to healthcare? You could try walking over to him and saying, "I demand that you treat me! I have a right to your services." Somehow I don't see that going over too well though.

You could try offering to give him something in return for him doing you the favor of treating you, but that would be a voluntary exchange - or private, fee-for-service healthcare.

Outside of that, you only have two options for getting this doctor to treat you: 1) you could kidnap him and physically force him to treat you against his will, or 2) you could vote to create a government that would do the forcing for you. But you'll notice one major problem with these scenarios - they both violate the rights of the doctor.

Now let's compare that to a couple of the rights acknowledged in our Bill of Rights - the Freedom of Speech and the Freedom of Religion. If you go back into that remote forest where there's no government, can you speak your mind? Of course you can - just open your mouth and start talking. Would you be able to practice your religion? Sure. You don't need help from anyone to do either of those things.

Granted, other people can participate in both of those activities with you. But they aren't *required* for either of them. For anything to be a true right, you have to be able to exercise it on your own.

You've heard the cliche philosophical question, "If a tree falls in the forest and no one's there to hear it, does it make a sound?" Here the answer is much, much easier. If you're in the middle of a forest and no one is there to help you can you still exercise your rights? You bet! No question about it.

Exercising a right must not take from another person:

As you just saw, exercising a natural right must not require the participation of another person. On a similar note, exercising a natural right must not require you to take another person's property. You can exercise your rights all day, every day and that won't limit anyone else's ability to exercise their rights at all. They are an unlimited resource.

For example, I have chosen to use my right to free speech to write the book that you are reading right now. I spent a lot of time putting it together and writing down my ideas. In fact, I'm probably somewhere exercising my free speech even as you are reading this. But even though I've been very active in using my rights, that has absolutely no impact on your freedom to write a book on whatever topic you want. And if you write a book, that doesn't mean that your neighbor can't use his free speech to express his ideas however he wants. We can all exercise our rights to the fullest extent and no one else in the world is worse off because of that.

What's wrong with this picture?

If I went to another person and forced him to work against his will to build a house for me, we would call that slavery. But if I go to the government and ask it to force another person to work longer hours so he can pay higher taxes to provide me with a house, we call that public housing.

Now lets turn our focus to that idea of health care as a right. Clearly, healthcare is not an unlimited resource. There are a limited number of doctors and a limited number of hospital beds. So if I exercise my "right" to health care and I'm checked into the hospital, that could possibly mean that there isn't a bed or a doctor available for you to exercise your "right".

In other words, my exercising my "right" to healthcare would take from the amount of "rights" available for other people to use.

Natural rights are an unlimited resource and are very unique in the fact that you can exercise them to fullest extent possible and still guarantee that your neighbor will have the opportunity to exercise them just as much as you.

Exercising a right must not require the government to grant you that right:

As we discussed earlier, our rights are part of our humanity; we have them the moment we are created. Clearly, the government has nothing to do with that process. How could it? What can the government possibly do to change something that is part of our nature?

Look at it this way - what would happen if Congress passed a law tomorrow that said, "From this day forward, no citizen who is born shall ever be greedy"? Absolutely nothing. The tendency to be greedy is a part of human nature and Congress has absolutely no power to change that. In the same way, a government has no power to pass a law that says, "All people shall be born with a right to free speech." That right is a fundamental part of our nature as human beings, whether our governments like it or not.

This is an important concept to understand, because just as the government has no legitimate authority to prevent us from exercising our natural rights, it has no power to grant us new rights either (ie. change our human nature).

The next time you see a politician on television talking about how he is going to grant people the right to do this or that, you know that he's full of it. Governments cannot grant rights, they can only grant privileges that can be taken away whenever the government chooses to.

ANOTHER VIOLATION: THE MYTH OF COLLECTIVE RIGHTS

Over the years, the experts have been very effective at popularizing the belief that groups of people can have rights collectively. The problem is, this idea violates the basic principles of natural law and - as you will see - it is completely incompatible with freedom.

But if these collective rights do exist, the experts need to be able to answer a few questions about the nature of collective rights. As we discuss these questions, we'll use the idea that unions have collective bargaining "rights"[4] as an example of a collective right.

> **Man holds these rights, not from the Collective nor for the Collective, but against the Collective—as a barrier which the Collective cannot cross;... these rights are man's protection against all other men.**
>
> — Ayn Rand
> The Ayn Rand Column

[4] A "right" to Collective Bargaining is the idea that employees who are represented by a union have a right to demand that their employer negotiate with them as a group.

Question 1: Who grants collective rights?

You might recall that our individual rights are granted to us by God. Who granted collective bargaining rights to these unions? Unions were not created by God[5] or nature - they were created by people.

The experts might claim that the government or the union itself grants collective rights, but that's a really dangerous proposition. If the government or a union can grants rights, then it can take them away just as quickly. In that case, what we're talking about here isn't really a right but a privilege.

Question 2: What limit is there to what rights can be granted?

If the government or the union is able to grant collective rights, is there a limit on the kind of rights they can grant? Could the government grant union members the right to drive 20 mph over the speed limit without getting pulled over? Or could it grant union members the right to use the 20 Items or Less Lane at the grocery store even if they have a full cart? If we're going to be in the business of granting rights, let's at least have some fun with it!

Question 3: When are collective rights granted?

Our individual rights are granted to us the moment we are created and they are a part of our humanity. When is a person suddenly granted collective bargaining rights - at the moment he joins a union?

In that case, this person doesn't have a right at one point in his life. Then after he joins a union he miraculously gains this new right. But when he leaves the union, he loses it again. That doesn't exactly sound like an unalienable right that can never be taken away. In fact, it sounds an awful lot like a privilege.

Question 4: How can one person have more rights than others?

Personally, I am not a part of a union. So there's no way that I have collective bargaining rights. But, according to the experts, the members of some unions do. If all men are truly created equal, how can union members have more rights than I do? In any system where collective bargaining rights exist, some men are seen as more valuable than others in the eyes of the government.

---

[5] If you aren't a religious person you may choose to believe that our rights are granted by nature. In that case, all of the arguments in this book will still apply exactly the same way logically. However, it is my personal belief that our rights are granted to us by God.

To be clear, if a union wants to negotiate with an employer on behalf of its members it is more than welcome to do so. But a union does not have a right to demand that the employer negotiate with it and no one else. If the employer doesn't want to negotiate with a union, that is his choice.

Remember, the employer has a right to associate with whomever he wants and a right to contract with whomever he wants. When union members demand that they have a right to collective bargaining, what they are saying is that the employer in question should be stripped of his right to liberty. In this case, they believe the union's rights should take precedent over those of the employer.

Which brings up another major problem with the concept of collective rights. If the collective has rights and individuals have rights, there will be a lot of situations where those rights come into conflict with each other. In those cases, whose rights take precedent?

If you ask nearly anyone who believes in collective rights, they will tell you that the rights of the collective take precedent.[6] That means if you exercising your rights is considered harmful to the group, then your rights will have to be violated.

Let's use President Teddy Roosevelt as a mainstream example of how this works. In 1910, he gave a speech called "The New Nationalism" where he said:

> **"[E]very man holds his property subject to the general right of the community to regulate its use to whatever degree the public welfare may require it."**

What he's saying here is, the government ultimately has the right to tell you how you can and can not spend your money - and if necessary, the right to take it away from you. In fact, later in the speech, Roosevelt claims that you should only be allowed to create property if the way you create it is considered to be a benefit to the rest of the community. Put more simply, the interests of the collective are of the highest importance.

Where does that leave you as an individual? It makes you expendable. You are no longer unique and sacred as a human being. You are just one interchangeable piece that makes up the whole. If you get in the way of the community getting what it wants, then your rights are going to have to be violated.

Take Roosevelt's logic just one step farther. His argument is that it's

---

[6] For example, in Socialism and Democracy Woodrow Wilson wrote that:

"[State socialism] proposes that all idea of a limitation of public authority by individual rights be put out of view, and that the State consider itself bound to stop only at what is unwise or futile in its universal superintendence alike of individual and public interests."

In the following paragraph he goes on to claim that: "Men as communities are supreme over men as individuals."

acceptable to violate an individual's property rights if that would be beneficial to the country as a whole. If that's true then why stop at property rights?

His argument is that sometimes it's acceptable to violate one person's rights for the benefit of everyone else. If that's true, then why is slavery wrong? Slavery is simply the complete violation of one persons's right to liberty for the benefit of another. Based on Roosevelt's rhetoric, if it would be in the public interest for you to lose your right to liberty and be forced to work for the benefit of someone else, then we almost have a *duty* to do it.

> "Without property rights, no other rights are possible. Since man has to sustain his life by his own effort, the man who has no right to the product of his effort has no means to sustain his life. The man who produces while others dispose of his product, is a slave."
>
> — Ayn Rand
> Virtue of Selfishness

You might find this example to be absurd, but this kind of scenario is exactly why it is dangerous to put the interests of the collective ahead of individual rights. It diminishes us as human beings and makes us expendable.

HOW DO WE SEE INDIVIDUAL RIGHTS REFLECTED IN THE CONSTITUTION?

It would be easy enough to just point to the Bill of Rights here and then move on wouldn't it? But come on! That's no fun. Let's be more creative than that.

Instead, let's explore the fact that the entire structure of our government was designed to protect individual rights. That is why the Founders gave us a constitutional republic and not a democracy.

Yes, you read that right - the United States is not a democracy. You've probably heard a thousand times that we are a democracy and democracy is the greatest thing since sliced bread. But this is one more area where our modern experts have intentionally misled us.

In reality, democracy is a terrible idea that always fails. I know that might be tough to believe after years of hearing that democracy is wonderful. So don't take my word for it; here is what James Madison had to say about it:

> **"Democracies have ever been spectacles of turbulence and contention; have ever been found incompatible with personal security; and have in general been as short in their lives as they have been violent in their deaths."**[7]

That's not exactly a ringing endorsement.

Democracy is pure majority rule - everyone gets a vote and whatever 51% of the people want to do, they can do. There's a popular analogy that demonstrates exactly why that's so dangerous:

> **"Democracy is two wolves and a sheep voting on what to have for lunch."**

How do you think that's going to work out for the sheep? Probably not very well. In this scenario, his rights are not respected and he has nothing to protect him from the will of the majority. That's the problem with democracy - it does nothing to defend the rights of the minority and inevitably degenerates into mob rule.

On the other hand, a constitutional republic has a variety of mechanisms that protect the rights of people who aren't in the majority. There are quite a few ways that a constitutional republic can protect the minority, but for the purpose of this book we are going to focus on just one.

The most interesting way that our Constitution protects the rights of the minority is that it originally required taxes to be applied to everyone the same way. In Article 1, Section 8, it says:

> **"... all Duties, Imposts and Excises shall be uniform throughout the United States;"**

This is a brilliant way to protect the rights of the minority. Imagine how this would have worked in the early days of this country when duties and excises[8] were the main form of taxation for the federal government. In that situation, the people in the majority can't impose a tax on the minority unless they are willing to impose that same tax on themselves. That naturally protects people in the minority from having crushing taxes laid solely on them.

So in the previous example, the two wolves wouldn't be able to have the sheep for lunch unless they were willing to have a bear come along later and eat them too! That would probably make them think very carefully about how they treated that sheep - even though the sheep was in the minority.

---

[7] Federalist #10

[8] Duties are taxes on the import or export of products and excises are taxes on the sale of products.

But since the 16th Amendment[9] was ratified and we started imposing an income tax, we've gotten further and further away from this idea. Not surprisingly, we are paying a price for removing this protection for the rights of the minority. If nothing else, it has made it much easier for Congress to grant tax loopholes to corporations and special interest groups. Because those organizations can get favorable treatment from the government, they are willing to spend incredible amounts of money on lobbying and campaign donations.

All of that makes our representatives much more concerned with pleasing those corporations and special interests than they are with protecting anyone's individual rights - let alone the rights of those in the minority.

As you can see, these topics of rights and the mechanisms in a republic to protect them are much more than just academic concepts. They have a very real impact on the quality of your life and the size of your bank account.

Ok - we covered a lot of ground in this chapter. But the most important concept you need to remember is that our rights are given to us by a much higher authority than just a man-made government. Because of that, Natural Law demands that our governments respect our rights. If they don't, we cannot expect to be prosperous or free.

[9] As we discussed in the last chapter, the 16th Amendment granted Congress the power to impose an income tax and removed the requirement that direct taxes be applied proportionally based on the population of each state.

Could you at least ask permission before trying to run my life? Thanks!

Principle 3: A legitimate government must have the consent of the governed

THE MASS OF MANKIND HAS NOT BEEN BORN WITH SADDLES ON THEIR BACKS, NOR A FAVORED FEW BOOTED AND SPURRED, READY TO RIDE THEM LEGITIMATELY, BY THE GRACE OF GOD."

— Thomas Jefferson
Letter to Roger C. Weightman
June 24, 1826

I magine that you are stuck on a deserted island in the middle of the Pacific ocean. After living on the island for several weeks you've learned to fend for yourself and have completely given up on being rescued.

Then, out of the blue, I show up on the island. (I know - talk about taking a bad situation and making it worse!) As soon as I get there, I tell you, "I'm in charge here and you are going to live under the rules that I make." How would you feel about that arrangement?

Something tells me that you wouldn't be too thrilled about being forced to live under my rule-making. Nobody would be. Common sense tells us that it is wrong for one person to tell another person what to do against his will. For exactly the same reasons, it's wrong to force a system of government on a group of people without their permission.

But now that you and I are on the island together, how do we know who should be in charge?

As we've established throughout this book, you and I are equal so there is no natural justification for one of us to rule over the other. In other words, neither of us is born "superior" to the other and destined to lead. The only way to solve this problem that is consistent with Natural Law, is for the two of us to come to an agreement on how to govern our affairs on the island.

The principle here is that for any government to be legitimate, it must have the permission of the citizens to govern.

SO WHAT? WE ALREADY HAVE A GOVERNMENT...

For us today, it's easy to disregard this idea. We already have a government so we won't be authorizing a new one any time soon. It feels like this doesn't affect us at all. But this principle is of paramount importance - not just because it is a part of Natural Law - but because of what it tells us about the nature of government itself.

If the laws of nature require a government to have the consent of the governed before it can be legitimate, that tells us that the power of government is - and *must be* - limited. It is limited to only exercising those powers that the people have agreed to - and nothing more. Beyond that, this idea of consent doesn't just mean that the people must agree to create the government when it's established.

The source of political power

If a government must have the permission of the people in order to be legitimate, that means that there are no powers that a government just has naturally because it's a government. All powers a government has must first be granted to it by the people.

In other words, the people are the source of all legitimate political power.

It means that the government is required to abide by the terms of the agreement for as long as it is in operation.

Think about what happens if you have a contractor come in to do some work on your house - for instance to remodel your kitchen. The contractor will come into your home to take a look around, then he'll tell you what he can do and give you a proposal for what work needs to be done. Assuming you like the proposal, you agree to it and give the contractor the authority to make those limited changes to your house. As long as he sticks to doing the work you agreed to, everything goes along just fine.

But what would that situation look like if the contractor believed he could grant himself the authority to do other things after you agree to the proposal (like our government believes it can)? You initially invited the contractor in to remodel your kitchen. But after he gets about half-way into the job he thinks, "While I'm here I might as well do the bathroom too. Oh, and I bet a sunroom would look great on the back of the house." He could go through your house finding everything that needed to be "fixed" or improved and turn your life into chaos - or worse. Just let your imagination run wild with what he could do to your house... and your wallet. You would lose complete control.

Does that sound like a positive situation? And this is only your house. A contractor doesn't have anywhere near the power to screw up your life that a government does. That's why government must be strictly limited to only doing what the people have consented to. Otherwise, our entire society quickly becomes something similar to the illustration with that contractor.

If the government doesn't need the consent of the governed then there is no way to limit its power. Government be-

> "Sometimes it is said that man cannot be trusted with the government of himself. Can he, then, be trusted with the government of others? Or have we found angels in the forms of kings to govern him?"
>
> — Thomas Jefferson
> First Inaugural Address

From time to time you'll hear the argument that the government doesn't need the consent of the governed because people aren't capable of governing themselves. This is also a justification for a lot of the laws that restrict what you do in your personal life - you might make a bad decision so you need the government to protect you from yourself.

But if we aren't capable of governing ourselves, why would we assume that the people in our government are capable of governing everyone? Or have we found a race of people who are better than the rest of us and never make poor decisions?

comes the ultimate authority - politicians can then grant themselves any powers they want for any reason. After all, they don't need your approval. The government can do whatever it wants with you or to you - and there's nothing you can do to protect yourself. Your life is in their hands.

As you can see, this is a very simple concept - in a world where all men are created equal it's impossible for a person to have a natural born mandate to rule over another person. The only justifiable way to create a government is to get the permission of those who will be governed.

Despite how basic this idea is, our government violates it constantly and the violations are getting worse every day. We'll put the bulk of our focus for this chapter on just one of those violations - allowing executive agencies to create laws.

HOW HAVE THE EXPERTS VIOLATED THIS?

The way our government was originally designed, the only way to create a law was for Congress to pass a bill and then the president would sign it into law.[1] One hundred percent of the responsibility for creating the laws that we live under was given to parts of the government who were elected by the people they were intended to serve.

The House of Representatives and the president were accountable to the people and the Senate was accountable to the States.[2] That gives you and me as citizens the power to have a say in the laws that we live under. If our representatives pass laws we don't like, we can throw them out of office and elect new representatives who will pass laws that we do like. In that way, we are continually able to give our consent to what our government is doing.

But today, the vast majority of our laws are not passed by Congress - they are created by executive agencies. If you're not familiar with executive agencies, they are the alphabet bureaucracies that you hear about on the news all the time (the EPA, FCC, FDA, IRS, and on and on). These agencies operate as a part of the executive branch of government and they are supposed to help the president in executing laws that have already been passed.

At this point you might be asking, "Wait a minute. I thought Congress was supposed to pass laws - how is it Constitutional for executive agencies to create laws?" Good question. Allowing executive agencies to create laws is blatantly unconstitutional. But our modern experts have come up with a few ways to justify it and the Supreme Court has upheld it.[3]

Let's look at two of the justifications for executive agency lawmaking that I've seen come up most often.

[1] Yes I realize that the president could veto the bill and then Congress could over-ride his veto. But let's keep this simple for now.

[2] Our Senators were originally appointed by the state legislators. That was changed by the 17th Amendment in 1913 and now our Senators are elected directly by the people. The 17th Amendment was probably as destructive to our freedom as any single act in our nation's history.

The way our federal government operates has a major effect on our states. So the Senate was supposed to be their voice in Washington, D.C. That limited how big the federal government could get because the Senate (ie. the states) would never agree to pass legislation that would allow the federal government to infringe on the power of the states. Because of that, there was a natural limit to how big the federal government could get.

Shortly after the 17th Amendment was ratified, the federal government started to grow by leaps and bounds into the giant we see today. There's no doubt about why that happened - a major Constitutional check on federal power (the Senate) was removed.

[3] It's important to note that just because the Supreme Court rules on something, that is not the final word on whether or not it is consistent with the Constitution. The justices on the Supreme Court are only human and it's entirely possible for them to be wrong. In fact, they've been wrong on numerous occasions throughout our history. That is just one more reason why it's important for citizens like you and me to understand our rights and the Constitution.

1. Executive agencies don't pass laws.
They issue regulations.

This one is just silly. Changing the name you put on something doesn't change the substance of what you are actually doing. This would be like arguing that a new law wasn't a violation of the 1st Amendment because it didn't in infringe on your "freedom of speech" - it just "stopped you from talking about stuff." The effect is still the same.

If you want to see for yourself that regulations are just laws by another name, look at it this way. Do you have to follow the regulations that are issued by executive agencies like the IRS and the EPA? Of course you do. And if you don't follow one of these regulations, will someone from the government either fine you or put you in prison? Yes they will.

So they're laws.

2. Congress can delegate its power to other areas of government.

This is probably the most common excuse you'll hear for why it's ok for executive agencies to pass laws. The argument the experts make goes something like this: yes, Congress does have *all* the power to create laws in this country.[4] But if it wants to, it can delegate some of that power to other areas of the government. In other words, if Congress doesn't want to take responsibility for making the laws about a certain issue they can just have someone in the executive branch do it for them (ie. executive agencies).

The problem with that is, the Constitution does not grant Congress any authority to delegate power to other branches of government. This is an idea that the experts have simply made up out of thin air. The citizens of this country have entrusted the different branches of our government with specific types of power. No one in government ever has the authority to alter who has permission to use that power.

Here's why. Have you ever had to be out of town for a week or so and needed to have someone come over to your house to feed your dog and pick up your mail? Most likely you have. So a few days before your trip you meet up with a friend to give him a key to your house and a list of the jobs you need him to do for you.

How would you have felt if you got back from your trip and found out that your friend had never actually gone over to your house? Instead, he made a few copies of your key and gave them to other people around

---

[3] Article 1, Section 1 of the Constitution states that "All legislative power herein granted shall be vested in a Congress..."

What that means is, Congress has all of the power to create laws for our federal government."

[5] http://www.carolinajournal.com/exclusives/display_exclusive.html?id=8762!

[6] http://www.theblaze.com/stories/2012/02/17/exclusive-2nd-n-c-mother-says-daughterss-chool-lunch-replaced-for-not-being-healthy-enough/

your neighborhood. Then those people were the ones who went over to check on your house.

I don't know about you, but I would have been all kinds of angry. He violated your trust. You gave your friend the key because you trusted *him* to go in your house - not so that he could decide who *else* could go into your house. He has no business making those kinds of decisions - it's your house. Only you have the authority to decide who gets to go inside.

Government works on the same principle. As citizens, we entrust our government with some of our power so that it can accomplish a few jobs for us. But the bottom line is that it is our power - only we get to decide who uses it. In this case, we gave Congress the power to make laws - not the power to decide who *else* should be able to make laws.

To reiterate that point: It is *our* power as citizens that the government is using. Only we get to decide who uses it.

But when it comes to executive agencies, we didn't consent to who is using our power. The people running our government took that power for themselves. Not only that, but we also have no realistic way to give our consent to what these executive agencies are doing. Did you get to vote for the bureaucrats who are making the laws at the EPA?

Consent of the governed?

Most of the laws we live under right now are passed in a way that we as citizens didn't give our consent to, by agencies that are unaccountable to us. Where exactly does the consent come in?

How about at the FDA? Or the HHS? Of course not. If they pass laws that we don't like, there is virtually nothing that you and I can do as citizens to hold them accountable.

This is a major violation of Natural Law. I'm sure by now you know that there are consequences that come along with that. Let's look at just one.

Executive agencies tend to be the source of our most ridiculous laws - as well as the laws that are most likely to control personal aspects of your life. Because they know that they don't need approval from you and me, the people who run these agencies feel comfortable passing laws that members of Congress wouldn't dare to pass.

That's how we get to a situation where a preschooler can be harassed by school officials because the lunch she brought didn't meet federal guidelines. Yes, that actually happened. In 2012 a little girl from North Carolina brought a lunch to school that her mom had packed for her, but officials at her school replaced that with food from the cafeteria.[5] Apparently, a salami and cheese sandwich on wheat isn't "healthy" enough according to the Department of Agriculture.[6] (While we're on the topic, why in the world is the Department of *Agriculture* making regulations about school lunches?)

So now the federal government literally has rules for what you can and cannot pack in your child's lunch. And if you don't follow those rules (that you probably didn't even know existed), they will replace your child's lunch at your expense and send your child home confused about why mommy or daddy doesn't give them good food.

Can you imagine the people of this country giving their consent to a law that allows government officials to rummage through the lunches that our children bring from home? There is no way that would happen. That's why anyone with the power to pass laws must be directly accountable to the citizens who are affected by those laws.

Unfortunately, the school lunch regulation is only one example of thousands of completely absurd laws that we now live under. And our laws are only going to get more and more absurd until we start following Natural Law and give citizens the opportunity to consent to the laws they live under.

> **The government is now making rules for what you have to give to your child for lunch. Does that sound like the definition of freedom that we talked about earlier in this book?**

HOW DID WE GET HERE?

The method of creating laws through executive agencies is nothing like the process laid out in the Constitution. So you might be wondering, "How is it possible for us to get so far off track?"

The answer to that goes back to President Woodrow Wilson (1913-1919). Wilson thought the world of the early 1900s was a lot more complicated than the world of the Founding Era. Because of all the new technology and the complexity of the economy, he argued that the old-fashioned process of having elected representatives vote on every piece of legislation didn't work anymore.

In an article called *The Study of Administration*, Wilson laid out his vision for a new administrative state. Under his new system, an army of

---

[5] http://www.carolinajournal.com/exclusives/display_exclusive.html?id=8762!

[6] http://www.theblaze.com/stories/2012/02/17/exclusive-2nd-n-c-mother-says-daughtersschool-lunch-replaced-for-not-being-healthy-enough/

unelected experts who were specially trained in both a specific field of science and the art of governing would be responsible for creating our laws. Under Wilson's theory, because these people were unelected they would be free to make decisions based on objective science instead of politics.

Once Wilson became president, obviously he began to put his plan for an administrative state into action. Over the years, other presidents like Franklin Delano Roosevelt and Lyndon Baines Johnson moved our country in that direction as well and - slowly but surely - Wilson's vision has become a reality. The executive agencies that now make most of our laws work very much like what Wilson described in *The Study of Administration* over 100 years ago.

Unfortunately for you and me, Wilson's vision violates Natural Law and ignores human nature.[7] So his plan hasn't created a super-efficient government where well-meaning administrators make the best decisions for society based on the latest science. Instead, it has given us an over-sized federal government run by an elite political class that is increasingly detached from the rest of the country and looks out only for it's own interests.

J.W. HAMPTON, JR. & CO. V. UNITED STATES (1928)

One of the cases where the Supreme Court upheld this idea that Congress can delegate it's legislative power to executive agencies was in *J.W. Hampton, Jr. & Co. v. United States*. This case in particular is worth looking at because it highlights an important aspect of what the experts have done to our Constitution over the last century.

In his opinion upholding the Congressional delegation of power in this case, Chief Justice William Howard Taft[8] said this:

"If Congress shall lay down by legislative act an intelligible principle to which the person or body authorized to [exercise the delegated authority] is directed to conform, such legislative action is not a forbidden delegation of legislative power."

The key here is that Taft argues that the Constitution doesn't forbid Congress from delegating power to executive agencies. And that's true. There aren't a whole lot of actions the Constitution forbids the

[7] It violates Natural Law by allowing administrators to make laws without the consent of the people. It ignores human nature by assuming that these administrators will be above self-interest (ie. that they will always do what's best for the country and not what's best for themselves, even though they aren't being held accountable).

[8] If that name feels familiar to you, that's because it is. You're probably more used to seeing him referred to as President Taft. William Howard Taft is the only person in U.S. history to be president and then go on to serve as the chief justice of the Supreme Court.

government from taking. The reason for that is, it was written from the point of view that the government doesn't have the power to do anything unless the people grant it that power. Whether or not the Constitution forbids Congress from delegating power is almost entirely irrelevant. What Taft should have been looking for if he wanted to be true to the Constitution is a clause that *grants* Congress the authority to delegate power.

Do you see what Taft has done there? Not only did he give the Court's approval to an obviously unconstitutional act by Congress; but he also created a precedent for future courts to use that implies that the government can do anything it wants unless the Constitution says otherwise. That is the complete opposite of the mindset that the Constitution was written from.

With this ruling he is helping to create the general perception that we don't have a government that can exercise a handful of powers that are laid out in the Constitution. Instead we have an all-powerful government that has been forbidden from taking just a handful of actions. After decades of experts pushing that idea, many of our public

People create governments; not the other way around. If we - as creators - don't grant a power to the government, where exactly does that power come from?

officials now believe that they can do anything they can dream up as long as the Constitution doesn't specifically say they can't.

Unfortunately, your freedom won't last long in a nation that is run by politicians with that mindset.

HOW IS CONSENT OF THE GOVERNED USED IN THE CONSTITUTION?

Perhaps the best illustration of how this principle is used in the Constitution is the mindset that it was written from. If you read through the entire document, you'll notice that it spends much more time on explaining what the government *can* do than what it *can't* do.[9]

That's because the assumption was that the government had the power to do absolutely nothing... until the people granted it power. It has no intrinsic powers that are just there because it is a government.

---

[9] In Article 1, Section 9 and Section 10 the Constitution does lay out a handful of actions the federal government and the states are forbidden to take.

A great example of this mindset is Alexander Hamilton's objection to the Bill of Rights. One of the arguments against the Constitution when it was originally written was that it didn't have a section that listed specific rights that the federal government was forbidden from violating. Hamilton didn't see the point of that. As he explained in the Federalist #84:

> "For why declare that things shall not be done which there is no power to do? Why, for instance, should it be said, that the liberty of the press shall not be restrained, when no power is given by which restrictions may be imposed?"

Clearly this statement comes from the perspective that the federal government had absolutely no powers except those that were granted to it by the people.

Here's a great way for you to visualize this concept. If you're a parent, did you ever have to sign a permission slip for your child before he could go on a field trip? When I was in school we needed a permission slip for just about anything. Even if we wanted to take an aspirin between classes we needed to bring in *written proof* that we were allowed to do it.

The Constitution works the same way - it is our written permission slip to the government. This permission slip basically says, "We the people, give the government permission to use this list of powers - but no more." Just like it was assumed that your child couldn't go on the field trip until he could prove otherwise, it should be assumed that the government cannot do anything until it can provide written proof (in the Constitution) that it has permission from the people to use that power.

Someone remind me, why did we create this government?

Principle 4: The primary purpose of government is to protect our rights

In the last chapter, we discussed the fact that any legitimate government requires the permission of the governed. That brings up an interesting question: Why would anyone agree to live under a government in the first place?

To find out let's go back to our deserted island for a little while - only now, it's not so deserted. You and I have managed to make a pretty nice life for ourselves on the island. Other people like what we're doing and they are starting to join us. How did they find out about us? I have no idea but just go with me.

Anyhow, there are now 10 of us living on our not-so-deserted island. We are all perfectly free. No one can tell us what to do. There are no laws, no regulations, nothing. We can all exercise our natural rights as much as we want. So why would we ever create a government?

Here's the problem - you have gotten particularly good at creating useful products out of the resources on the island. You have the softest bed, the most food, and the most comfortable clothes. But every time you leave your hut, people steal your property and try to imprison you. The only option you have left is to spend most of your time sitting on your porch with your coconut cannon desperately trying to protect yourself and your property.

In that situation, even though you are completely in control of your rights - you aren't able to *exercise* them because you are so busy *protecting* them. That problem isn't isolated to you either. On some level, everyone else on the island is going through a similar experience of being on guard 24 hours a day.

After a few months of going through that, it would make sense for you to go to a few of the other people and say, "I am wasting all of my time trying to protect my rights. It's almost all I do! We should work together and create a government that could protect all of our rights so that we have some time to go gather food and live our lives."

To do that, you might start by drawing up some basic rules for the island - no one is allowed to go into someone else's hut and take their property, no one is allowed to physically harm anyone else, etc. Then, you might decide to put some money together and appoint one of the islanders to be a police officer who could go around and make sure everyone is following the rules.

Once you get that going, you could even establish a little island court system. Then, if someone did steal some of your property the police officer could help you find out who did it and take them to court so that you could get repaid.

Now that you have confidence that you aren't 100% responsible for protecting your own rights, you can leave your hut to go out to gather some food and actually start to live your life.

The reason we create governments is to protect our rights. Not to create a strong economy, to give people health care, or to promote fairness. As odd as it sounds in a world where we've been brought up to look to the government as the solution to all of our problems, **the primary purpose of government is to protect the individual rights of citizens.**

There are two other lessons we can learn from this island example as well:

1. Good laws should make you more free, not less free

> "[T]he end of law is, not to abolish or restrain,
> but to preserve and enlarge freedom."
>
> — John Locke
> The Second Treatise of Government

The purpose for creating laws is not to restrict your actions, but to make you more free. At first glance, this seems counter-intuitive - how could something that tells you what you can't do make you more free?

Take a look at the previous example. The people on our island were so preoccupied with protecting their rights that they couldn't do anything else. But once a law was created to prohibit stealing that gave everyone the ability to leave their homes and actually start exercising their rights. That law gave them *more* freedom.

As citizens, we should consider this whenever our representatives are proposing new legislation. Would the new law make you more free or less free?

2. The government did not grant us our rights

> "Life liberty, and property do not exist because men have
> made laws. On the contrary, it was the fact that life, liberty,
> and property existed beforehand that cause men to make
> laws in the first place."
>
> — Frederic Bastiat
> The Law

If you read Chapter 3 on the nature of our rights then you already know that our rights are a part of us as human beings. The government had absolutely nothing to do with giving them to us. Nonetheless, this illustration should help you see even more clearly the relationship between citizens and a legitimately created government. The government was created to serve us and protect our rights - it works for us.

As citizens, we have a government because we first had rights. Not the other way around.

HOW ARE THE EXPERTS VIOLATING THIS IDEA?

Sadly, the vast majority of what our government is used for today violates the primary purpose it was created for. The government we have today - which was created to *protect* our rights - has now become the greatest *violator* of our rights.

An entire book could easily be written just detailing the countless ways our government violates our rights - it's happening every single day. However, for the purpose of this book we're going to limit ourselves to only discussing three examples of how that is happening.

The government is violating our rights any time it is used to:
1) to protect us from ourselves,
2) to create "equality", or
3) to create a strong economy.

1. Using government to protect us from ourselves

Today's experts are increasingly under the impression that the main job of government is to protect us from ourselves. They argue that we are likely to make bad decisions and we need someone to look out for us. Think seat belt laws and helmet laws. You might not make the right decision, so the government needs to step in and *force* you to do what's in your best interests.

The experts who make that argument miss the fact that true freedom means having the freedom to make bad decisions. People make poor choices every day - that's a part of life. The problem with writing laws to prevent you from making bad decisions is, who gets to decide what is considered a "bad" decision?

A lot of times people know they are making what others would consider a "poor" decision. But they are willing to do it because - for them - the possible benefits are worth the risk.

For example, there are a lot of motorcycle riders who understand exactly how dangerous it is to ride without a helmet. But they love the freedom of being out on their bike so much that, if riding without a helmet means that they might smash their head on the pavement at some point, they're just fine with that. In my opinion that's a stupid decision to make, but then again, it's not my head getting smashed.

It's not the experts' heads that are in danger of getting smashed either. So they are in no position to decide whether that risk is worth the reward of riding down the highway with the wind in your face.

If we are all created equal, why should the experts decide for the rest of us what a happy and fulfilling life looks like? After all, what reason do we have to believe that their judgement is superior to our own?

Clearly it's not possible for the experts to tell you the best way for you to live your life. But just for the sake of argument, let's assume for a moment that they could. Even if the experts could prove what you were doing was harmful to you, they still have no authority to protect you from yourself. There are a couple of reasons why:

But what about insurance?!

Some experts will make the argument that motorcyclists not wearing a helmet will lead to more injuries and a rise in insurance costs. But that is really an issue for the helmetless rider and his insurance company to deal with - not the government.

You might say, "But if that knucklehead rides without a helmet he could raise MY insurance rates - doesn't that violate my rights?" No. If you don't like the fact that your insurance company covers helmetless motorcycle riders, then you are free to do business with another company. What you aren't free to do is use the government to take away another person's right to liberty.

IT IS IMPOSSIBLE FOR A PERSON TO VIOLATE HIS OWN RIGHTS.

It is completely impossible for you to violate your own rights. Try to imagine for a moment how that would work. How in the world would you force yourself to do something against your will? How could you steal your own property?

By doing something that you choose to do, you are exercising your right to liberty - even if the activity you choose is harmful to your body or your life. In the end, it is your body and your life. What you decide to do with them is up to you.

> "The sole end for which mankind are warranted, individually or collectively, in interfering with the liberty of action of any of their number, is self-protection... [T]he only purpose for which power can be rightfully exercised over any member of a civilized community, against his will, is to prevent harm to others. His own good, either physical or moral, is not a sufficient warrant... The only part of the conduct of any one, for which he is amenable to society, is that which concerns others. In the part which merely concerns himself, his independence is, of right absolute. Over himself, over his own body and mind, the individual is sovereign."
>
> — John Stuart Mill
> On Liberty

Mill makes a brilliant point here. When you are engaged in an activity that affects no one but yourself, no one else in society has the authority to stop you.

The rest of us in society might think we're doing what is best for you, but that's not a good enough justification. After all, if we're all equal then how can we say with certainty that we are right and you are wrong?

The only justification in Natural Law that anyone has for using force to restrict your actions is to prevent you from violating someone else's rights.

Sure, if you and I are friends and I see you behaving destructively I might choose to step in and talk you out of it. But I have no authority to use force to stop you against your will.

Despite that, we have experts all over this country who think it is their job to tell you the best way to live. The most popular way to do that in recent years has been to try to "encourage" you to eat healthy food. Whether that means banning large cups of soda, banning trans fats, or taxing junk food, the experts want to have a say in what you eat.

But if I love junk food and I eat a lot of it, that's not a violation of my rights. It's just an example of me living my life in a way that other people don't approve of.

If I choose to live my life by eating cupcakes until my belly explodes, that's my problem. Maybe that's my idea of a happy life. Maybe in my mind being able to gorge myself on cupcakes is the pinnacle of achievement in life. Who are these experts to butt in and rob me of my glory?!

In that scenario, I am using my Right to Liberty to create what I feel is the most fulfilling life possible. Just because other people might believe that the effects of my decisions will do harm to me, that doesn't mean I am violating my own rights. I simply choose to use my life and my body a different way than they do.

Remember, the proper role of the government is to protect our rights. So in a situation where no one's rights are being violated, why is it getting involved?

PROTECTING ME FROM MYSELF IS IN ITSELF A VIOLATION OF MY RIGHT TO LIBERTY.

"Let People alone, and they will take Care of themselves, and do it best; and if they do not, a sufficient Punishment will follow their Neglect, without the Magistrate's Interposition and Penalties."

— John Trenchard
Cato's Letters #62

In other words, if we just leave people alone to run their own lives they'll do it better than anyone else can. And if they don't, amazingly enough, nature will punish those people on its own without the government getting involved.

In the example to the left, some experts would likely argue that society can't just sit back and allow me to eat myself into a cupcake-filled oblivion. My actions could seriously endanger my life - and they have a duty to prevent me from violating my own Right to Life. But even if that were true, it makes no sense to destroy one right in order to save another. (In this case, the government would be destroying my Right to Liberty in a misguided attempt to save my Right to Life.)

If I am engaging in a voluntary activity, then I am exercising my Right to Liberty - even if that activity might be harmful to me. When the government comes in and tells me that I can't do something that I choose to do - even if it is trying to do what's best for me - that is a violation of my Right to Liberty.

2. Using the government to create "equality"

"The law can be an instrument of equalization only as it takes from some persons and gives to other persons. When the law does this, it is an instrument of [theft]."

— Frederic Bastiat
The Law

Most of our modern experts believe that it's the job of government to make sure that the rich don't get too rich and the poor don't get too poor. While our Founders focused on creating a nation that offered equal opportunity, today's experts are preoccupied with creating equal outcomes.

That's why you'll hear them use phrases like "narrowing the wage gap," "leveling the playing field," and "making the rich pay their fair share." Regardless of how they phrase it, the goal is to make everyone in society equal from a material standpoint.

But let's think about that for a moment. If you are going to ensure that everyone in society has roughly the same amount of wealth, what will you have to do? People have different talents, ambitions, and skill sets and it's a fact of life that they will all achieve different levels of success. So if you are going to create material equality, eventually you will have to take money away from one person in order to give it to someone else.

Obviously, that would be a violation of the first person's property rights and of Natural Law. Because of that, any government policy aimed at creating material equality is destined to fail.

There is simply no possible way to create material equality without violating someone's rights. The only equality government can offer that is consistent with Natural Law is to protect everyone's rights equally, to offer equal justice, and to allow us to stand equally before the law. If a person violates the law, he should be judged using the same criteria and face the same penalty as any other person in society whether he's rich or poor, black or white, man or woman. That is the only equality that government can offer.

3. Using government to create a strong economy

There is a common perception that our politicians should constantly be taking action to make sure we have a strong economy with a lot of high-paying jobs. In fact, those two areas generally top the list of issues the American people want our federal government to deal with.

Unfortunately, there isn't anything our politicians can do to create long term prosperity. The only two actions a government can take that will benefit the economy are to maintain a positive economic environment and to protect our property rights.

It can create a positive economic environment by keeping taxes low and making sure that businesses aren't strangled by a maze of ridiculous rules and regulations. When taxes are low people know that they will get to keep the money that they earn. That gives them a greater incentive to go out and work hard or take a risk on starting a new business. More people working hard and becoming entrepreneurs is great for the economy.

By keeping the number of rules and regulations at a reasonable level, the government is making it easier to do business. The reason for that should be obvious. Look at it from a personal standpoint. Imagine that you are thinking about opening a business. But the government has set up a complicated and expensive system of forms and permits that you have to fill out before you can get started. Would that make you more or less likely to open your business? See, when you make it easy to do business, more people are going to do it. And when more people are getting into business, that's great for the economy.

The other major step a government can take towards strengthening the economy is to protect our property rights. No economy can become prosperous if everyone is constantly worried that all of the wealth they've earned can be taken from them at any time. Think about it - would you go through all the effort and frustration of building a business if you thought it could be taken away from you for no reason?

To help you see how this translates into the real world, look at what happened back in 2009 when General Motors and Chrysler were given a bail out. The government pressured those companies to terminate their contracts with thousands of car dealerships throughout the country. The process of selecting which dealers would lose their relationship was done seemingly at random and for a lot of them it did tremendous damage to the business that they had spent their lives building.

Imagine you are thinking about opening a car dealership - and creating all of the jobs and economic activity that goes along with that kind of investment. Would you be more or less likely to go ahead and open it now that you have seen that the government might arbitrarily decide to destroy your dealership and possibly take away your livelihood?

To put it all of this very simply, the best thing a government can do for the economy is to avoid putting obstacles in the way of creating wealth and to protect the right of the people to keep that wealth once they earn it.

Friedrich von Hayek explains the relationship between the government and the economy perfectly in his book *The Road to Serfdom*. It's a lot like the relationship between a gardner and a plant. A gardner can't force a plant to grow. All the gardner can do is create a positive environment for it to grow in. He can make sure the plant gets sunlight and has access to water, etc. But in the end, it's really up to the plant.

The government is in the same position. It can't force people to be ambitious and creative or to invent new products that people will want to buy. If we, as a nation, choose to be lazy and unproductive there's no law in the world that's going to turn that into prosperity. All the government can do is create a positive economic environment.

After that it's up to us whether or not we have a strong economy.

But once it has created that positive environment, what more can it do to strengthen the economy that wouldn't violate our individual rights? Almost all of the programs that are proposed today involve injecting money into the economy somehow - through stimulus programs or bailing out struggling companies, etc. And who's money is it that the politicians are injecting into the economy? It's *yours*.

In other words, what the government is doing with these stimulus programs is taking your money away from you and forcing you to invest in a variety of businesses. That's clearly a violation of your rights to liberty and property so it shouldn't come as any surprise to you that these programs never work.

"Oh," some experts will argue, "but we could use that stimulus money to invest in roads and bridges. Are you saying that the government can't spend money on infrastructure?!" No that's not what I'm saying. Building roads and bridges is certainly a legitimate function of government. However, the reason to build a road is because... you need a road. Not to create jobs.[1] Building a road just to create jobs is called "busy work". We're supposed to leave that behind in kindergarten. If we're going to waste money by having construction workers doing busy work, we might as well have them cutting and pasting snowmen out of construction paper.

When the government puts money into roads and bridges that don't need to be built or are being repaired solely for the purpose of stimulating the economy, that diverts resources that could be put to a better use. Remember, they are using *your* money to do this. If they didn't waste it on unnecessary infrastructure, that money would be in your pocket for you to use for your retirement, to educate your kids, or go on vacation.

On the other hand, let's assume for a moment that these roads and bridges, etc. really do need to be built or fixed. Creating that kind of infrastructure is one of the few jobs that our government is supposed to be doing (at least on a local level anyhow). If there is an epidemic out there of crumbling roads and bridges - so much so that fixing them will substantially effect our economy - then shouldn't we ask the same politicians who are proposing this idea why they weren't maintaining the roads to begin with?

The bottom line here is that these kinds of stimulus programs take money away from you and give it to someone else. That is a violation of your rights. If a government truly wants to create a strong economy, all it has to do is follow Natural Law. In this case, that means protecting our property rights and allowing people the greatest freedom possible to pursue their dreams.

---

[1] Henry Hazlit uses this example in his book Economics in One Lesson. I definitely recommend it for future reading.

By the way...

How is it that politicians never see the irony in calling for a stimulus that basically involves them doing a fundamental part of their job that they've been neglecting? What they are saying here is, "We haven't been doing our job for *years*. You have no idea how bad we've let these roads get. In fact, we've screwed up so badly that if we just go back and fix the mistakes that we've made as politicians, we're pretty sure that alone will turn the economy around."

HOW DOES THIS SHOW UP IN THE CONSTITUTION?

"The powers delegated by the proposed Constitution to the Federal Government, are few and defined. Those which are to remain in the State Governments are numerous and indefinite. The former will be exercised principally on external objects, as war, peace, negotiation, and foreign commerce; with which the last power of taxation will for the most part be connected. The powers reserved to the several States will extend to all the objects, which, in the ordinary course of affairs, concern the lives, liberties and properties of the people; and the internal order, improvement, and prosperity of the State."

— James Madison
Federalist #45

This one's pretty simple. The powers granted to the federal government in the Constitution are all designed to protect your rights.

If you want to get a good idea of what the size and scope of our federal government was intended to be, it's important for you to know the primary role it was supposed to play in this country. **The purpose of the federal government was to create a peaceful and secure environment for the states to operate in.** That's it.

You might be thinking, "That doesn't sound like it was supposed to do very much." You got it. The federal government was designed to have very little - if any - impact on your daily life. But look around and see how often it is involved in your life today. That alone will tell you how far we've gotten away from the original intent of the Constitution.

Virtually all of the powers that were originally granted in the Constitution fall into four main categories: national defense, foreign trade and diplomacy, immigration, and allowing products to move freely throughout the country. You'll notice that all but one of those categories deal with issues that are **outside** of our nation's borders - just like James Madison mentions in the quote at the beginning of this section.

Let's look at how each of the four main categories of federal power are intended to protect your rights.

National Defense:

This isn't exactly a tough one. This category would include all the powers related to raising an army and a navy, declaring war, etc. Obviously, these powers are intended to protect your rights from foreign threats.

This is an area we want the federal government to handle for us because all of the states working together provide a much stronger defense than each state trying to protect itself individually.

Foreign Trade and Diplomacy:

The main powers the federal government has here are setting tariffs on imports and exports, making treaties, appointing ambassadors, and receiving ambassadors from foreign nations. There are a variety of ways the government can use these powers to protect your rights. For example, they can be used to maintain peace with other countries, to protect your property rights from foreign threats, or they could even be used to ensure that other countries respect your rights when you travel or do business abroad.

We want this to be handled at a federal level because it's important for our nation to speak with one voice. If we had all 50 states trying to negotiate different policies on their own it would be a chaotic mess and greatly reduce the government's ability to use this power to protect your rights.

Immigration:

This should be another obvious one. This category would include the power granted to the federal government to create uniform rules for... wait for it... *immigration!* This power can be used to protect your rights by making sure that the people who come into this country aren't carrying dangerous diseases and aren't criminals who pose a threat to you and me.

This is a role for the federal government because there is simply no effective way to handle it at the state or local level. When you allow all 50 states to create their own immigration policy - the actual policy is being set by the state with the lowest standards for immigration. Think about it. If you wanted to come to the U.S. but you were denied entry by the state you would prefer to live in, what would you do? Most likely, you'd figure out which state had the lowest standards and enter the country there. Then, once you were in the country you could easily move to the state you originally wanted to be in.[2]

[2] James Madison discusses this in detail in the Federalist #42.

Maintaining one common economic market throughout the country:

We finish up with the only significant area where the federal government can exercise power inside the nation's borders - maintaining one common economic market throughout the country. Having a nationwide free market like this is very helpful in creating a strong economy. But that is actually a side-benefit.

The primary benefit is that the powers in this category serve to protect your rights. Let's look at a few of them. In the Constitution, Article 1, Section 8 grants Congress the power to:

"coin Money, regulate the Value thereof, and of foreign Coin..."

In other words, Congress would have the authority to issue the one type of money that would be accepted throughout the entire country. This definitely makes it easier to do business in this country. I used to live on the Iowa/Illinois border and we were always crossing into Iowa to go shopping or go to a baseball game. Can you imagine what it would be like if every time we crossed the border we had to stop and exchange our money? Or if we had to constantly hold on to two different types of money? It would make life a whole lot more complicated.

But of greater concern for the Founders were the opportunities for fraud that would be created if states were allowed to create their own money.

The most obvious possibility for that is counterfeiting. With a variety of different currencies floating around it would be hard for the average person to keep track of what was real money and what wasn't. All of that confusion would make it easy for counterfeiters to take advantage of folks from out of state.[3]

Another possibility for fraud was that individual states might intentionally devalue their own currency. When a state devalues its money, it means that whatever money you have will buy less today than it did yesterday. So the $100 bill you had in your pocket yesterday might have been enough to buy a nice pair of shoes... then all of a sudden, that same $100 bill will barely buy a gallon of milk today. Because the state lowered the value of its currency, any money you might have is now worth much, much less.

It doesn't matter whether a crook is trying to give you fake money or a state is destroying the value of money you already have - either way you are having your property stolen from you. By having the federal government create one type of money for the entire country, the Founders were trying to minimize those risks and protect your right to keep your property.

---

[3] Even though the concerns of the Founders surrounding the coining of money might be a little hard to relate to they were certainly justified. In the years after the American Revolution there were significant problems with counterfeiting and states devaluing their money. Those issues cost a lot of people huge sums of money.

Why in the world would a state devalue its own currency?

Sometimes, a government will take on more debt than it can handle. That may be hard to believe considering we live in a country that was over $16 trillion in debt as of 2012 - but trust me it happens. When a government realizes that there's no possible way to pay off the debt it has acquired, one of the only ways to pay it off is to devalue its currency.

One method of devaluing currency is to just print a whole lot more of it. Look at it this way - why is DaVinci's painting of the Mona Lisa so valuable? Because it's a one of a kind. But what if he had painted two of them - then how valuable would they be? Not quite as valuable. What if DaVinci had spent his whole life only painting and re-painting that same portrait and there were thousands of them floating around? Then they wouldn't be worth much at all.

Currency works in a very similar way. If a government prints a lot of it, it is worth less and less. So let's say a government has $1 million in debt that it can't repay. One option that government has is to start printing more currency. Before long, that same $1 million might only be valuable enough to pay for a cup of coffee. At that point, paying of the original debt is no problem at all!!

If you've been watching the news, you may have noticed that the United States has been printing a whole lot more money over the last 5 to 10 years. What do you think that means for the money you have in your bank account?

A little later in Article 1, Section 8 the Constitution grants Congress the power to:

"promote the Progress of Science and useful Arts, by securing for limited Times to Authors and Inventors the exclusive Right to their respective Writings and Discoveries;"

This power gives Congress the authority to create a system where people are able to secure legal ownership over their ideas and inventions. If you write a great book or produce a popular movie, this prohibits other people from copying your work and profiting from it. This is important because it enables the government to protect your right to keep your property that isn't as tangible and obvious as your car or your house.

For this power to be effective, it has to be granted to the federal government. Otherwise, you could have problems where certain states might not recognize a copyright that you had from another state. In that case, someone could simply steal your work, then go across state lines and profit from it. That would make your original copyright virtually worthless and destroy your right to the property you had created.

For one last example, Article 1, Section 8 grants Congress the power to:

"regulate Commerce [...] among the several States..."

This part of the Constitution gives Congress the power to ensure that products and services are able to move freely and easily throughout the country. Not only does this allow the federal government to facilitate the nationwide free market that we discussed earlier, it removes one of the most likely causes for states getting upset with each other and destabilizing the union.

The type of scenario the Founders were afraid of is something where one state would place a duty (tax) on products that are imported from a neighboring state. Then the second state might get upset and retaliate with a higher tariff on goods from the first state. That could easily be the beginning of a trade war; and trade wars often lead to real wars. For our union to work the bonds between the states had to remain strong. Because of that the Constitution prohibits states from placing taxes on its imports or exports.

This part of the Constitution protects your rights by allowing the government to create a peaceful, secure environment in which to exercise them. If we allowed friction to grow between the states and weaken our union, it will be much less effective in protecting your rights.

Obviously, this power needs to be granted to the federal government because only it can create rules that will govern then entire country.

Notice that all the the powers we just discussed help the federal government perform its role of creating a peaceful and secure environment for the states to operate in. Just as importantly for this chapter, they do that without violating anyone's rights. Nothing in the Constitution authorizes the government to violate anyone's liberty or to take something from one person in order to give it to another person.

In this way, the Constitution is consistent with the Natural Law principle that the primary purpose of any just government is to protect individual rights. Knowing that goes a long way towards helping us understand the limits of our federal government. It tells us that any interpretation of the Constitution that would allow the government to violate our individual rights is almost certainly wrong.

That's not the only guidance Natural Law gives us about the limits on government power either. As you'll see in the next chapter, no government can legitimately have the power to do anything that you and I can't do as individuals.

It's a crime when the government does it too...

Principle 5: The government cannot have the power to do anything you can't do as an individual

"THIS POWER THEREFORE, WHICH NO MAN HAS, NO MAN CAN TRANSFER TO ANOTHER."
— John Trenchard
Cato's Letters #60

One thing that we know to be true about governments is that people create them. If nothing else, we can look back to the creation of our own country to prove that. We can read the letters and notes from our Founders as they were discussing what type of government we should have and what power it should be granted. In this country, a group of people got together and wrote a Constitution that established the government that we live under today.

It's not as if there was some independent, all-powerful government lurking around this part of the world just waiting to create the people who would live under its rule. That's crazy talk. We know that governments cannot create people. People create governments.

I know this is common sense and it probably seems a little silly that I'm going over it in such detail. But knowing that people create governments tells us a lot about how much power a government can legitimately have.

Because of the fact that people create governments - and all of a government's power comes directly from the people - **the government cannot have the power to do anything that you and I can't do as individuals**. The reason is very simple: You cannot give something you don't have.

Look at it this way - I would really like to give you $1 million right now. But why can't I do that? Well... because I don't have $1 million dollars. It's not possible for me to give you something I don't have. That same logic applies to government. We can only grant it powers that we already have as individuals.

I know this sounds really odd at first - especially when we live in a world where it feels like the government has an overwhelming amount of power. But if you stick with me for the next few pages - I promise - you'll see that this is the only logical way to organize a government. Not to mention the only one that is consistent with Natural Law.

The area of our lives where this concept is easiest to recognize is our individual rights. As we discussed in Chapter 3, no one has the authority to violate the rights of another person. Because of that, it is also true that the government cannot have the authority to violate a person's rights.

To illustrate this idea for you, let's go back to the deserted island for a little bit. Imagine you're on a deserted island minding your own business when all of a sudden I show up again (I promise I'm not stalking you, it's just a wild coincidence.). Would I have any authority at all to decide that I was going to imprison you for no reason (ie. violate your right to liberty)? Of course not. No one ever has the right to violate the rights of an innocent person.

But... what if I bring a friend with me this time and the two of us decide that you should be imprisoned. Do two people have the authority to violate a person's rights? What if I bring two friends? Or ten? Or one million? Would one million people have the authority to put you in a prison for no reason and throw away the key? Of course not. It doesn't matter how many people are involved - it's never ok to violate someone's rights.

Now let's assume that when I come to your deserted island I bring ten friends with me. Once we get there we decide to organize ourselves into a government. Then, we vote to grant ourselves the power to imprison you against your will. Would that make it ok?

It seems obvious to us that one person can't force another person to do something against his will. For some reason, we make the same question so much more complicated when the term "government" is involved. But we have to ask ourselves - if a government does have the authority to violate someone's rights, where did that authority come from?

Whenever we are discussing what a government should or should not be doing, the first question we need to ask is this: "If I were to take this action as an individual citizen, would it be a crime?" If the answer is yes, then that action is almost certainly something the government doesn't have a legitimate authority to do either.

There is nothing inherently special about a government that gives it the power violate someone's rights. It isn't created by God or by nature. Governments are created by people and run by people. So if a government claims to have the authority to violate a person's rights it needs to answer this question: What exactly is the source of that power? It certainly can't come from the people because they don't have that power themselves. And again, it's impossible for people to give something they don't have.

Remember that any legitimate government must have the consent of the governed. Imagine that I walk up to you and say:

"Hey, a few other people and I are starting up a new government. It's totally going to oppress you and violate your rights. So what do you say, are you in?!"

I'm going to go out on a limb and say that you wouldn't agree to be a part of our new country. It's unreasonable to assume that people would knowingly give their consent to a nation that violates their rights.

SO THEN WHY BOTHER CREATING A GOVERNMENT?

All of that brings us to the question: "If the government can't have the power to do anything I can't do as an individual then what's the point of creating a government in the first place?"

Well, a government doesn't need to have new and different powers to do its job. Remember, the purpose of government is to protect our rights. As individuals, we have the authority to protect our rights as well. But when we work together as a society to protect everyone's rights we can do it much more effectively and efficiently. As we discussed in the last chapter, when you aren't 100% responsible for protecting your own rights, that allows you to shift your focus to actually exercising them.

Let's look at an example of how combining our power as individuals can be used to create an effective government.

If someone were to break into your home and threaten your life, you have a right to defend yourself. That seems pretty straight-forward, right? If someone poses an immediate threat to your rights, you most definitely have the authority to defend them.

But what if your neighbor hears the commotion in your house and decides to come help you out - would he have the authority to do that? (In this scenario we're assuming there's no government.) Sure he would. It wouldn't require him to violate anyone's rights. In fact, he's actually taking action to defend someone's rights - so he would be perfectly in line with Natural Law.

You and your neighbor would have a much easier time fending off the burglar as a team than you would all by yourself. Even better than that would be if the entire neighborhood came over to help you protect your home. With the help of the whole neighborhood you would easily be able to protect your rights from the burglar. Simply by combining our power as individuals, we can accomplish things that would be extremely difficult to do alone.

If you take that hypothetical example of a neighborhood coming together to protect your home and expand it out to an entire country, that's where you get the government's authority to handle our national defense. When we come together to defend ourselves as a nation we are much more powerful than all of us working individually. And creating that extra power doesn't require the government to do anything that we could not do as individuals.

Now consider a scenario that is just a little different. What if the burglar broke into your house when you weren't there and stole your TV (again, assuming there's no government) - then what would you do? Chances are you'd do your best to figure out who took your TV so you could get it back and hold the thief accountable. That's what I would do anyway. And I would be well within my authority to do so.

Would there be any problem with you asking your neighbor to help you track down the thief? Not at all... well, assuming that he's not the one who stole your TV. Then it would be a pretty awkward conversation, wouldn't it? Anyhow, your neighbor would be perfectly justified in helping you get your TV back for all the same reasons we just talked about in the previous example.

Take that example of having your TV stolen and move it into the real world. What would you do if someone actually broke into your house and stole your TV tomorrow? You would call the police and have them help you figure out who stole it. Once you figure out who the thief is, you would take him to court so that you can get your TV back and hold him accountable for his violation of your rights.

In that example, what have we done? We've taken your authority under Natural Law to protect your right to property, combined it with everyone else's power and used it to create a police force and a court system that can help you use your power more effectively. You are still going to try to track this thief down and hold him accountable, but now you aren't responsible for doing it all by yourself. That allows you to continue to focus on other aspects of your life.

As you can see from these examples, new and expanded powers aren't required for a government to do its job properly. We just need to combine our power as individuals in a way that enables us to provide better protection for everyone's individual rights.

HOW ARE THE EXPERTS
VIOLATING THIS CONCEPT?

You might be thinking, "Ok, this whole idea that the government can only use power that I have as an individual is nice as an academic exercise but it doesn't have anything to do with real life. I don't know anyone who thinks the government should be able to throw innocent people in prison for no reason." That may be true - but we allow our current government to violate people's rights in other ways all the time.

For example, imagine that I broke into your house and stole $100 out of your dresser. Then I immediately took it down the street and donated it to a homeless shelter. What would that be called? Theft. Plain and simple. You have a right to keep the property that you've earned. I have no business going in and taking it away from you - even if I think I have a good reason for it.

How would that situation be any different if - instead of going into your house and taking your money myself - I voted for a politician who had the government take your money on my behalf... and then gave it to the homeless shelter? The effect is still the same. Your property has still been taken from you and given to the homeless shelter. The only difference is that in the second example I asked the government to commit the theft for me.

You say, "There's a huge difference. In the second example you didn't just barge into my house. You went through the government and did it legally." That's true, but just because something is legal and approved by the government, does that make it moral?

Let's say I go through all the proper legal process and have a law passed that would allow me to throw you in prison for no reason. Would that be ok? If we don't have a problem with using the government to violate someone's Right to Property, why can't we use it to violate someone's Right to Liberty?

The bottom line is that even if you are taking money away from someone for a good cause, it is still a violation of that person's right to property. You are taking property from the person who earned it and giving it to someone else. As we demonstrated with the example of me breaking into your house, it would be a crime if I did that as an individual. So where does the government get the authority to do it?

To refer back to our island example, how is it wrong for a random group of 10 people to come along, take your property, and then donate it to charity - but as soon as we give that group the label of 'government', suddenly those same actions are acceptable?

Are you saying we shouldn't do anything to help homeless people?

Of course not. We all have a responsibility to help out those who are less fortunate in society.

However, we shouldn't expect the government to do it for us and we shouldn't use the government to *force* others to donate to charity. Private charities are able to do a much better job of addressing these problems and at a lower cost.

Not only do private charities offer us a much more effective way to help people in need, they are also able to do it without violating Natural Law.

Besides, if we aren't willing to help the homeless unless the government forces us to do it, what does that say about us as a society?

BUT I PAID INTO THE SYSTEM!!

These kinds of social welfare programs clearly violate our right to property, and yet we have well over *100* of them in this country.[1] In fact, the primary function our federal government serves today is to take money away from some Americans and give it to other Americans that our politicians feel are more deserving.[2]

More than half of the money spent by our federal government violates Natural Law. So as a country we are actually better at violating Natural Law than following it. And we're paying for that in numerous ways.

But before you get upset, you should know that one of the programs that will cost us most dearly is one that you might support: Social Security. You say, "Social Security?! But it's not a welfare program." Unfortunately, it is. While Social Security is the most popular of our social welfare programs, it's also the most misunderstood.

A lot of Americans don't have a problem with Social Security because, when they receive their Social Security check they've been led to believe they are just getting back money that they paid into the sys-

[1] http://www.cato.org/doc-download/PA694%2Epdf?uri=public%3A%2F%2Fpubs%2Fpdf
%2FPA694%2Epdf

[2] Approximately 65% of our federal spending from 2001 - 2010 went to entitlement programs (ie. welfare programs). http://shadow.foreignpolicy.com/posts/2012/05/22/obama_s_
legacy_on_afghanistan

tem. The sidebar on the next page shows you why that isn't true. But even if it were, this program would still violate Natural Law.

Let's assume that I break into your house and take money out of your wallet again. Only this time I take it downtown and open up a retirement account for you. What would that be called? Theft. Even though I have the best of intentions, I have no authority as an individual to force you to save for your retirement. If it would be theft for you or me to do that, then where exactly does the government get this authority?

Even though Social Security claims to be doing what's in your best interests and most Americans see this program as harmless, it still violates Natural Law. It's very popular and a lot of Americans love it, but the consequences of enacting Social Security will be very destructive - as is always the case when we violate laws of nature.

FREEDOM = CHOICE

Remember from our first chapter that freedom means being able to make choices. With Social Security you are told how much money you must contribute to your retirement and where you have to put that money. Even if you'd rather use that money now to pay for college or invest in something that provides a better return, you don't have those options. Is the Social Security program offering you more freedom or less?

Social Security is not insurance

A lot of Americans are under the impression that Social Security is a form of insurance. We are led to believe that our payroll taxes are put into a nice little trust fund that sits there and gains interest until we need it for our retirement. But that's simply not true.

Actually, the fact that it's not an insurance program was one of the justifications the Supreme Court gave for upholding it as Constitutional:

> "The proceeds of both the employee and employer taxes are to be paid into the Treasury like any other internal revenue generally, and are not earmarked in any way."
> — *Helvering v. Davis* (1937)

In other words, the Social Security tax you pay can not in any way be considered an insurance premium - it's the same as every other tax you have to pay. Dr. Clarence Minion did a great job of breaking down exactly what that means:

> All federal taxes, income taxes, estate taxes, gasoline taxes, and social security taxes, go indiscriminately into the same general fund of the federal treasury. From that general fund, Congress makes periodic appropriations for all the purposes of the federal government, including payments for social security benefits.

> Congress could continue to collect the so-called social security pay roll taxes even though Congress discontinued all social security benefit payments. Congress could wipe out the social security pay roll taxes and yet continue to pay all present social security benefits out of the general tax receipts of the federal treasury.

> Any apparent connection between the collection of social security pay roll taxes and the payment of social security benefits is purely coincidental. The Supreme Court has held that Congress is without Constitutional power to establish such a connection.*

That tells us a lot about what kind of program Social Security actually is. Unlike an insurance premium, the fact that you contribute payroll taxes gives you no legal right to receive benefits.** The government can raise the retirement age or change your level of benefits at any time, for any reason. In fact, if Congress chooses to it could eliminate your benefits altogether. As Milton Friedman explains in his book *Free to Choose*, your hopes of receiving a Social Security check rest entirely on the willingness of the next generation to impose taxes on themselves to pay for your benefits.

The only real difference between Social Security and other welfare programs is the way that our politicians have sold it to us. They have been very effective in convincing us that we are receiving insurance benefits that we've earned rather than a welfare check. Unfortunately, Social Security is just one more program where the government takes property from one group of people in order to give it to another group of people.

* http://www.fee.org/the_freeman/detail/the-social-security-tax#ixzz2Ob29OsHL
** http://www.ssa.gov/history/nestor.html

One problem with Social Security is that it has given the politicians an easy way to grab power for themselves by dividing Americans. Think about it - as soon as anyone suggests cutting government spending, what is one of the first responses we hear from D.C.? Politicians run breathlessly to the first available camera, put on their concerned face and say, "If we cut spending like that we'll probably have to cut Social Security benefits. Why do the people proposing these cuts hate senior citizens so much?"

What it has become is a tool for the politicians to threaten the American people any time we try to limit the size of government. Politicians who give us the sob story on Social Security are basically saying, "Don't you dare threaten my power or I will take away your retirement." In retrospect, how smart was it for us to give the government that kind of control over our lives? Arming the politicians with this ability to blackmail our seniors with threats of a diminished retirement has made it virtually impossible for us to limit the growth of the federal government.

That brings us to the second consequence of Social Security that we're going to go over (obviously there are plenty more) - the cost. Because of the way that Social Security is designed, the only way it can be sustainable is if there are always a lot more workers paying into it than there are retirees drawing benefits. With the baby boom generation retiring, though, we are at a point where there are only about 2 workers paying into Social Security for every retiree drawing benefits.[3] That creates a huge problem. A $16 trillion problem to be exact.

As of this writing, we have made promises to pay out $16 trillion in Social Security benefits that we don't have the money to pay for.[4] That is *in addition to* the $16 trillion national debt that you've heard politicians talk about. To put that into perspective, our yearly gross domestic product[5] is only $15.5 trillion.[6] So even if we confiscated everything that everyone in this entire country produced for an entire year, we still couldn't pay out the Social Security benefits we've promised.

All of that means that we are forcing the next generation of Americans to accept a much lower standard of living than we have enjoyed in order to pay for our retirement. And that's a best case scenario. When you add our unfunded Social Security benefits to the $16 trillion national debt, as well as the promises that we've made through Medicare and Medicaid, the financial consequences we're facing will likely be much, much worse.

---

[3] http://www.cato.org/publications/commentary/social-security-follow-math

[4] www.usdebtclock.org!

[5] Gross domestic product is the value of every product and service produced by a country.

[6] www.usdebtclock.org

Social Security is just one example of how our government is attempting to use power that you and I don't have as individuals. There are over 100 more social welfare programs that take money from one American in order to give it to another. Is there any wonder why Washington D.C. is so dysfunctional?

So are you saying we should just eliminate Social Security?

No. Our government made a promise to people and I believe we have an obligation to honor that. Many Americans have planned their future around Social Security and it's not fair to change the rules on them in the middle of the game.

However, we do need to begin to phase this program out. We should let the people who are now entering the workforce know that Social Security is ending and that they will be responsible for their own retirement. That way the program will still be there for those who have been counting on it but no new expectations will be created.

This does cause a problem in that younger Americans will be footing the bill entirely for the last generation of people who receive Social Security benefits. That is a violation of their property rights, but this is the least destructive way to get us back in line with Natural Law. We have created a bad situation and there is just no easy way to get out of it at this point.

But I heard there was a special Social Security Trust fund...

Technically, that's true. But it doesn't have a bunch of money in there earning interest the way you would expect.

The politicians spent the money from the trust fund on other projects years ago. What they put in there in return were government bonds (ie. IOUs). Before any of the money in that fund can be spent, it will first have to be taken from the general taxes that the government receives just like any other federal expense. In theory, you can argue that there is a Social Security trust fund, but at this point it's more of an accounting gimmick than anything.

IT SOUNDS LIKE YOU'RE SAYING ALL TAXATION IS BAD...

As we've gone through this chapter, this thought may have crossed your mind, "Ok, it does make sense that the government shouldn't do things individuals can't do. But what about taxes?" After all, you and I can't go around taxing other people. But before the government can perform even the most essential functions like national defense, it's going to have to take in a certain amount of money. How is that supposed to work?

Taxation is a tough topic because it's true - you and I don't have the authority to go around demanding that our neighbors give us money. But, what we can do is ask for compensation for providing our neighbors with a product or service. We do that all the time. If you have a job, you expect your employer to give you money in return for the work you do.

> **"[I]n the ordering of our affairs we should make as much use as possible of the spontaneous forces of society, and resort as little as possible to coercion."**
>
> — Friedrich von Hayek
> Road to Serfdom

When we look at taxation that way it tells us a lot about how the government should tax and what kinds of projects it should spend that tax money on.

1. It tells us that when we are laying taxes we want to avoid forcing people to pay taxes to whatever extent that's possible. That's why I believe an income tax is a violation of Natural Law. With an income tax, a portion of our money is spent on our behalf and we have absolutely no choice in the matter. Our property is being confiscated from us. That creates the impression that the government has first claim on any money we earn and then we get the privilege of keeping whatever is left over.

So then how should we tax? One way would be to go back to a system of excise taxes and tariffs on imports and exports like the Constitution originally authorized. I would even go a step farther than that and exclude essential items like food and medicine from excise taxes. That would create a situation where citizens are given some level of choice in how much money they are willing to contribute in taxes. A person who truly did not believe in what our government was doing would not be forced to support it.

You might be thinking, "But with just a few excise taxes and tariffs the government isn't going to get much money." Yes - that's another feature of this plan. Without all of the excess money that an income tax provides, our politicians are deprived of the power to spend money on much of the wasteful nonsense that we now see from Washington D.C.

Believe it or not, our country survived just fine without an income tax until 1913 - the government was just a lot smaller. When the income tax was passed, the federal government's spending was only 2.48% of our yearly gross domestic product. In 2012 it was 24.33% of gross domestic product.[7] Can you imagine how much more money - and personal freedom - you would have if the federal government went back to spending 2.48% of GDP?!

I know that is a little frightening in today's world where we rely on government so much - but I promise the country wouldn't fall apart. We may have to live with a few less museums about the history of magic[8] and a few less historic buildings built out of legos[9] but I think we'll make it. Don't forget, we survived just fine like that for well over 100 years.

2. It tells us that the government should only be spending money on projects or programs that can benefit every citizen at any time. You and I do have the authority to ask for compensation after we provide our neighbor for a product or service. However, we can't demand that our neighbor pay us for a service that we provided to someone else.

Because of that, we want to make sure that anything we allow our government to do is generally applicable to the entire population at all times. Think of national defense. Everyone benefits from keeping our country safe. It doesn't matter if you are a man or women, black or white, rich or poor - we all benefit in the same way. On a more local level you could think of roads. We all have access to roads at any time and we all have the opportunity to benefit from them.

When our tax money is used in that way, government is not confiscating our property. It is simply asking us to be compensated for a service it is providing for us. But again, once government starts asking us to compensate it for services that are provided to other people, that's a different story.

When we look at the taxing power this way it means that all taxes have to be applied generally (they must be applied to everyone in the community in the same way). It also means that all tax money raised must be spent on projects that benefit the community generally (tax money can't be used exclusively to benefit a specific area of the country, a specific race or gender, etc.). That severely limits the power of our politicians to manipulate their office.

No longer can they divide the American people by saying, "You folks in the middle class aren't doing as well as you should because those evil rich

---

[7] http://www.usgovernmentspending.com/spending_chart_1902_2015USp_XXs1li011mcn_F0xF0f F0sF0l_Spending_in_20th_Century

[8] http://dailycaller.com/2011/12/20/top-ten-government-spending-at-its-stupidest/

[9] http://www.nationalreview.com/campaign-spot/341471/cut-lego-purchases-first-mr-president

people are taking it away from you. If you vote for me, I'll take more money away from rich people and give it to you." No longer can they sell out to special interest groups by saying, "If you can get me some campaign cash, I'll spend some money on programs that benefit your specific group of people." Instead, they'll be forced to treat us all simply as Americans and focus on policies that make the community better as a whole.

It's a part of human nature for people to both like having power and to be corrupted by having it. And once we get a little bit of power, we usually want more. Whenever we are creating a government, one of our main goals has to be figuring out how to prevent politicians from abusing the power they are granted and grabbing more power while they're in office. This approach to the taxing power is one of the single most effective ways for us to do that.

WHERE IS THIS IN THE CONSTITUTION?

At this point I wouldn't be surprised if you're thinking, "Ok Chad, I was with you until now. But you've really gone off the rails with this idea." It's easy to see why you wouldn't be completely comfortable with this idea - our politicians completely ignore it today and it's now popular to believe that the government is the answer to all our problems. But as you're considering all of this, keep in mind that this is one of the principles that this country was built on and made it great.

If we want this country to become great again, we need to start moving back towards those principles. There's no other option. After all, these aren't just a bunch of great ideas that someone came up with. They are the laws of nature so they aren't going to change.

Believe it or not, the Constitution does follow this principle. If you read through the Constitution as originally written and the Bill of Rights,[10] there is only one area where it grants the federal government the power to do something that you and I cannot do as individuals: eminent domain.[11] Not surprisingly, that has come back to haunt us.

Eminent domain is the power that a government uses to confiscate private property in order to use it for a public purpose. Let's say a government is building a new road, but a private individual owns a plot of land in the middle of the proposed route. Eminent domain might be used to take that land and ensure that the road could still be built.

---

[10] The first 10 amendments to the Constitution are called the Bill of Rights. All 10 were ratified in 1791 - just 4 years after the Constitution was signed.

[11] You could make an argument that the fact that the Constitution allowed slavery to continue is a violation of this principle. However, that's not really the government doing something individuals cannot do. Instead, the government was allowing individuals to do something they had no Natural Right to do. Whether or not you consider that a violation of this particular principle, it is definitely a violation of Natural Law. And as we discussed earlier in this book, our nation paid a tremendous price for that violation.

Our Constitution addresses eminent domain in the Fifth Amendment where it says:

> "...nor shall private property be taken for public use, without just compensation."

This clause does limit the government's power by saying that it must pay you a fair price if it uses eminent domain to take your property. So the government can't just confiscate your property, it has to buy it.

What's the problem with that? You and I don't have the power to force someone else to sell us their property. Imagine how you would react if I just walked up to you one day and said, "Hey I just bought your house. Here's some money... you and your family have 30 days to move out." There might be some words that would come to your mind that aren't appropriate for this book. But putting those words aside, if I was actually successful in kicking you out of your house, my guess is you would feel it was unfair and unjust.

Why is it any more fair or more just if the government kicks you out instead of a private individual? You might say, "It's different because the government was doing it to create a project that would benefit the whole community. It's not fair for one person to hold up everyone else." But remember, when we violate someone's rights we are treating them as less than human. Do we want to degrade a person as a human being just so that a road can be built?

According to our Constitution, the government does have the authority to do that through the power of eminent domain. Not surprisingly, our politicians have abused this power numerous times throughout our history. Probably the best known instance of this abuse was in the infamous 2005 *Kelo v. City of New London* case.[12]

But let's not get lost in this discussion of eminent domain. That is the *only* section of the original Constitution and Bill of Rights that grants the federal government the power to do something you and I cannot do as individuals. So this principle is not some idealistic theory that can never be applied to real life. Far from it. It's how our country was originally designed.

I completely understand that this principle can be a difficult concept to get your head around. I struggled with it myself for quite a while

---

[12] In the Kelo case, the city of New London, CT decided that it could raise more tax money if it kicked a bunch of families out of their homes and gave that property to a developer so he could build a shopping mall and some office buildings. So the town did exactly that. The families - some of whom had been in their homes for generations - sued to keep their property. Sadly, the Supreme Court of the United States ruled that the government getting more tax money is a sufficient "public use" to justify stealing property away from its rightful owner and giving it to someone else.

when the idea was first introduced to me. It's so foreign to everything we were taught about government when we were growing up. How could it possibly work?

But as we finish this chapter, take a moment and consider it a different way. If it's true that the government has the power to do things that you and I cannot do as individuals, then shouldn't we be able to answer these questions:

• Where did this extra power come from? Who granted it to the government?
• What is the limit on that extra power? If the government can violate our rights in some ways, how much is too much?

Earlier in the chapter we discussed the fact that it's not acceptable for a group of people to violate someone's rights - no matter how big the group is. That doesn't change just because we give that group of people the label of "government".

Umm... who's going to protect us from this government we just created?

Principle 7: We need a Constitution to protect our rights from the government

IT'S BEEN SAID THAT "A MAN'S INTELLIGENCE DOES NOT INCREASE AS HE ACQUIRES POWER. WHAT DOES INCREASE IS THE DIFFICULTY IN TELLING HIM THAT."

— Ronald Reagan
September 12, 1983

Power is a very tricky thing to deal with isn't it? It's a lot like radiation. When it's used properly and in the right amounts, radiation can cure cancer. But when too much of it gets concentrated in one place, it will destroy everything it touches - like with a nuclear bomb.

That is the greatest lesson of the 1900's - any time we allow too much power to be concentrated in a government the results will be catastrophic. We saw way too many examples of this over the last 100 years - Hitler, Stalin, Mao - the list goes on and on. Even today we see it happening in North Korea.

This brings us to the most difficult question to answer when it comes to creating a government that will protect freedom: how do we keep government power contained? If a government is left alone, it will always grab as much power as it can until some outside force comes along and stops it. That's because it's human nature for people to like power. And when they get a little bit of power, they usually want more. The people who run our government are no different. As soon as they get into office, it's human nature for politicians to want to increase their power.

So how do we give the government enough power to do its job of protecting our rights, but also make sure that we don't give the government too much power so that it is able to violate our rights itself?

You've probably heard the cliche question asked before, "How do you police the police?" Well here the question is, "How do you govern the government?"

THE FINAL PRINCIPLE: We must have a well-written
Constitution to protect our rights from the
government and politicians.

Governments will always get bigger and bigger and politicians will always grab more and more power until some outside force comes in to stop them. As citizens, we need to create a system that restricts this tendency to grow government through a written constitution. Otherwise the government that we created to protect our rights will quickly become the one violating our rights.

**"The natural progress of things is for liberty to yield
and government to gain ground."**

— Thomas Jefferson
Letter to Colonel Carrington
May 27, 1788

In the Federalist Papers, James Madison explained the problem this way:

"If men were angels, no government would be necessary. If angels were to govern men, neither external nor internal controuls on government would be necessary. In framing a government which is to be administered by men over men, the great difficulty lies in this: You must first enable government to controul the governed; and in the next place, oblige it to controul itself."[1]

To paraphrase this, if men were angels then everyone would treat each other nicely and we wouldn't need a government. But men aren't angels - so we need a government to help protect us from other people in society. And if we had angels to run our government for us, we wouldn't need to worry about the government abusing its power and oppressing us. But we don't have angels to run our government for us, so we also have to find a way to protect ourselves from the government.

So how do we protect ourselves from the government? The easy answer is, "You need to write a constitution." A written constitution serves as a permission slip that tells our politicians exactly how much power they are allowed to use. It anchors the government down and restricts its natural tendency to constantly get bigger and bigger.

But as important as it is to write a constitution, it is equally important to design it properly so that it will be effective in protecting your rights from the government it creates.

[1] Federalist #57

I'm confused. How did you get to this principle?

Common sense tells us that if we don't do anything to protect ourselves, there are bad people in this world who will violate our rights. As we discussed in Chapter 5, the main reason we create governments is to help protect us from these bad people.

If we know there are some bad people in regular society who would like to violate our rights - and all men are created equal - then we know that there are also going to be bad people in government who would like to do the same thing. We need to protect ourselves from both.

The only effective way to protect our rights from the government is with a well-written constitution that is based on Natural Law.

We create governments to help us protect our rights from other people and we write constitutions to help us protect our rights from the government.

HOW DO YOU GOVERN THE GOVERNMENT?

Even though writing a Constitution is a great start, we have to remember that many of our politicians are going to be determined to grab more power. They aren't going to let a few words on a piece of paper stop them. What we need to do is design our government in such a way that it limits itself.

The way we do that is to base our system on human nature - or the way human beings behave naturally. For example, we know that people tend to like having power. And once they get a little power, they usually want to get more. It's also human nature for people to be self-interested - or to take care of themselves and their family before they take care of others. People have been this way throughout history and they aren't going to change any time soon.

Because of that, it's a pretty safe bet that our politicians are going to worry about their own interests before they worry about you and me and that they will try to grab as much power as they can. It's just human nature.

Since we know that's what they are going to do, we want to use it to our advantage. The way we do that is to create a system where the efforts of our politicians to grab power and take care of themselves actually end up being what limits the power of government.

Think about what happens when an insect gets caught in a spider web. The more that insect struggles and tries to get free, the more entangled it becomes. In the same way, we want our government to be designed so that the more our politicians struggle to gain power, the stronger the limits on their power become.

SO HOW DO WE DO THAT?

The first strategy we can use to make the government self-limiting is to pit the politicians' love of power against itself. We do that by creating separate branches of government and then giving each of them different powers. In that situation, if one group of politicians wants more power they are going to have to take it from another group of politicians.

It's human nature for that second group of politicians to love power too, so when their power is threatened they are going to defend it. The harder the first group fights to get more power, the harder the second group is going to fight to defend their own. Each group of politicians ends up containing the other, which naturally limits the size of government.

The lust for power can be an overwhelming force. The only way to restrain it is with an equal and opposite force - someone else's lust for power. At the end of this chapter we'll go into more detail about how this strategy is used in our Constitution.

> "The Experience of every Age convinces us, that we must not judge of Men by what they ought to do, but by what they will do; and all of History affords us but few Instances of Men trusted with great Power without abusing it, when with Security they could. [...] For these Reasons, and convinced by the woful and eternal Experience, Societies found it necessary to lay Restraints upon their magistrates or publick servants, and to put Checks upon those who would otherwise put Chains upon them."
>
> — John Trenchard
> Cato's Letters #60

In other words, if our leaders think they can get away with it, it's pretty much a given that they are going to abuse their power. History has given us very little reason to believe otherwise. Because of that we have to put very strict limits on the people in our government. If we don't, it's likely that - at some point - our politicians will use that power to enslave us.

That is ultimately the point of this entire chapter:

We must always put checks on people who would otherwise have the power to put us in chains.

The next strategy we can use to make our government self-limiting is very simple, but extraordinarily effective. We need to require that our representatives live under the laws they pass. Our politicians need to know that every law they pass will be applied to them in the exact same way it is applied to us as citizens.

This is a powerful way to protect our rights because no politician in his right mind would vote to take away his own freedom. Look at it this way: over the years we have heard a lot of politicians talk about how we're all going to have to sacrifice to get through tough economic times. But during those times, how often have those same politicians voted to give themselves a pay cut? Or to limit their own perks? Never. It's amazing how they always seem to find a way to provide for themselves.

What we want to do with this strategy is use that self-interest to our advantage. If our politicians won't even take away their own perks, there's no way they would ever vote to take away their own rights. Under this strategy of forcing them to live under the laws they pass, if our politicians aren't willing to limit their own freedom, they can't limit yours either.

> "Power ought to be granted on a supposition that men will be bad; for it may eventually be so."
>
> — William Grayson
> Virginia Ratification Convention
> June 21, 1788

When we are writing a Constitution - or passing regular laws - we should do it from the mindset that our government is going to be run by crooks. It's important for us to have that mindset because if the government is around long enough, at some point we're going to be right.

That may seem unfair, but look at it this way: the United States has been around for over 220 years. Do you think over that time we've elected a few crooks? You'd better believe it.

So when we are granting power to our government, we want to do it the same way we would if we *knew* that we were giving that power to a crook. If that were the case, we would do our best to give the crook as little power as possible and place so many restraints on that power that it's almost impossible for him to misuse it. That way, when the eventual crook does get elected we've already protected ourselves and limited the damage he can do.

It would be nice to be able to trust our public servants, but our rights and our freedom are far too valuable to take that chance. We must always keep a healthy distrust of those in power. Thomas Jefferson put it this way:

> "In questions of power, then, let no more be said of confidence in man, but bind him down from mischief by the chains of the Constitution."
>
> — Thomas Jefferson
> The Kentucky Resolutions of 1798

HOW ARE THE EXPERTS VIOLATING THIS PRINCIPLE?

What would you say if I told you that back when the Founders' signed the Constitution that the sun rose in the south - not in the east like it does today? Hopefully, you would laugh at me and dismiss my claim as complete nonsense. The sun has always risen in the east. It would be silly to claim otherwise because the laws of nature do not change.

As we've seen throughout this book, our Constitution was based on a similar set of unchanging Natural Laws. Just like the sun still rises in the east, all men are still created equal and we are all still endowed by our Creator with rights to life, liberty and property. To claim that those principles are no longer true would be silly.

However, you will see experts on tv regularly making the claim that the ideas in our Constitution are old and outdated. Because of that, the Constitution doesn't mean the same thing today as it did when it was originally written. No, the experts tell us, our Constitution is a 'living document' that evolves and adapts to meet the changing needs of our modern society.

Under this theory of a "living document", our Constitution has no fixed meaning. Instead, the experts in our government are

> "All that progressives ask or desire is permission - in an era when 'development,' 'evolution' is the scientific word - to interpret the Constitution according to the Darwinian principle; all they ask is recognition that a nation is a living thing and not a machine."
>
> — Woodrow Wilson
> What is Progress?

I would argue that President Wilson is the father of this living document theory. In this quote, he's claiming that we should interpret the Constitution according to Darwin's theory of evolution. He believes that there is no fixed meaning. Instead, the meaning of the Constitution is constantly evolving and adapting to its surroundings. What it means tomorrow may be completely different than what it means today.

allowed to re-interpret it in a way that serves the country's needs at a given time. This is how we've gone from the Constitution we talked about in Chapter 5 that has the power to deal with four main issues to the country we have today where the government is involved in every aspect of our lives. The words in the Constitution didn't change, the experts simply reinterpreted them to give the politicians more power.

Can you already see the problem with this "living Constitution" theory?

It completely violates the principle that we need to place limits on the government to protect our rights from the politicians. If the politicians can just re-interpret the Constitution to mean whatever they need it to mean, then what real limit is there on their power? What is left to protect us from the government?

To help you see why that's so dangerous, let's do a quick illustration. Imagine that you've decided that it's time for your family to purchase a new home. So you go down to your local bank and talk to the loan officer to see if he can help you get financing. After looking over your financial records, the loan officer leans back in his chair and says, "I have the perfect product for you! It's called a 'living mortgage.' How this works is, you sign the contract to get a mortgage from our bank. Then, from time to time, our board of directors will re-interpret the loan to make sure that it meets the needs of our bank at that particular time."

Thinking quickly, you ask, "Ok. Does that mean I get to re-interpret the loan to make sure it meets my needs?"

And the loan officer tells you, "No. Only the bank can re-interpret the terms of the loan. The living mortgage will do absolutely nothing to protect you."

Would you sign up for a living mortgage? Of course not! You can easily see that this bank is just trying to take advantage of you. In this situation, that bank can do anything it wants to you and you have absolutely no protection.

The same is true with a living Constitution. This theory leaves you and me completely vulnerable to out of control politicians. Despite that, this is a commonly accepted way to view our Constitution in the legal world today.

You might be wondering why the experts would accept this theory if it's so bad. Well, why do you think the bank would think a living mortgage was a great idea? Because the bankers are the ones making the changes. A living mortgage puts them in complete control.

The same is true with the experts. The living Constitution puts them in control because they are the ones who will be doing the re-interpreting. So they can "re-interpret" themselves more power... at your expense.

WHERE DOES THIS PRINCIPLE SHOW UP IN THE CONSTITUTION?

Obviously one of the primary reasons for writing our Constitution was to limit the government and protect our rights. But there is a lot more to it than just that. The Founders created mechanisms like the ones we talked about earlier in this chapter that would force the government to limit itself.

For example, we discussed the idea of setting up our politicians' love of power to work against itself. That is the logic behind the separation of powers and checks and balances in our Constitution. Let's go into some detail about how that separation of powers works so that you can see just how brilliant it is.

For any government to function there are three jobs that it has to be able to perform. It has to be able to make laws, enforce laws, and judge laws. Without any one of those, the government will fall apart.

The reason why is simple. You and I could sit in my basement all day long writing laws. It's not going to do us any good, though, because we can't go out into the community and enforce them. Unless the two of us find a way to do all three of those jobs, our little basement government will fall apart.

What our Founders did in the Constitution was create three separate branches of government and gave each one a different job. It's not an accident that we have a legislative branch that makes the law, an executive branch that enforces the law, and a judicial branch that judges the law. The Founders set it up this way so that no one branch could run the government on its own. All three of them would have to work together before the government could function.

But let's say that one day the people in our legislative branch start feeling pretty good about themselves. We granted them some power and now they think they should have a little more. Remember, it's human nature for us to be tempted to feel that way.

With the functions of government separated the way they are, any time the legislative branch tries to expand its power it is going to infringe on the power of one of the other branches. But given what we know about human nature, what can we expect the politicians in the other branches to do? Their instinct is going to be to protect their own power and keep the legislative branch from growing.

In that way, our politicians' love of power is used to counter-act itself. The only way for one group of politicians to grab more power is to infringe on the power of another group of politicians.

However, you may have noticed that there's still a big problem with this design. What happens if the politicians decide to work together to grow the entire federal government? In that case there would be more

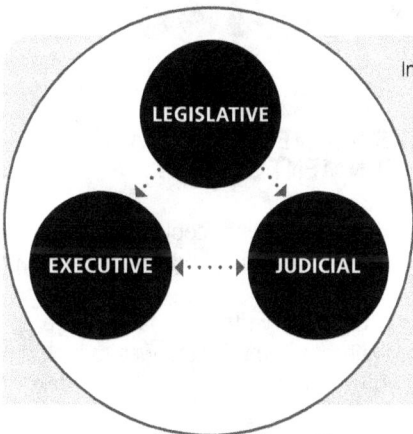

In this illustration - where the larger circle represents the power of the government as a whole - it's impossible for any one of the three branches to grow its power without running into resistance from one of the other two.

By designing our government this way, the Founders created a perfect equilibrium that keeps them all at the appropriate size.

power for all of them to share. How can we stop them from doing that?

The solution to this problem lies in the same idea of using power to counter-act power.

The 10th Amendment says:

"The powers not delegated to the United States by the Constitution [...] are reserved to the states respectively, or to the people."

That means *every* time that the federal government uses a power that is not granted to it by the Constitution, it is infringing on the power of the states. Now prepare for a shock... the people who run our state governments like power too. So their instinct is going to be to protect their power and keep the federal government from growing.

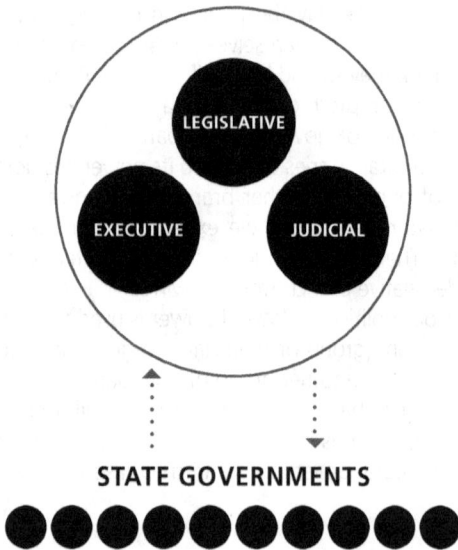

STATE GOVERNMENTS

IF ALL THIS WORKS SO WELL, THEN WHY IS OUR GOVERNMENT SO BIG?

"Ok Chad," you're thinking, "All of this sounds cool in theory. But in the real world our government is still getting bigger and bigger. Why isn't this working?" Great question.

The way our Constitution was originally written, Senators were appointed by state legislators. Their purpose in the Senate was to look out for the interest of the states. If you want to look at it in the context of this chapter, they were there to protect the state governments from the federal government.

Think about what that meant for any effort to increase the size of the federal government. Before you could give the federal government more power - which would take power away from the states - you would have to get the approval of the states first. How likely do you think the state governments would be to voluntarily give up their own power?

Unfortunately, in 1913 we ratified the 17th Amendment. That amendment changed our system to what we have today where Senators are elected by the citizens of each state. That means that the states governments no longer have a way to defend themselves from the federal government.

Now, the three branches of government have decided to work together to grow the entire federal government and there's not much the states can do about it. If you want to know why our government has gotten so big and out of control, most of the explanation for that lies in the 17th Amendment.

That is why it's so important that you're reading this book. Mechanisms like the separation of power and checks and balances do work to protect our rights from the government. But as citizens we must understand how they work and demand that our politicians respect them.

Unfortunately, over the years we have slowly allowed our politicians to break free from the chains that are placed on them by the Constitution. The way that we currently apply our Constitution no longer limits the power of our federal government in any realistic way. Because of that, we have lost a significant amount of freedom. Unless we once again step in and place strict limits on our federal government, we will continue to lose more and more.

The great news is, we already know how to do that. It's not as if we're desperately trying to find solutions to a problem that's never been solved before. We know how to limit government and we know how to protect freedom. We can return this nation to its status as the beacon of liberty for people worldwide. All we have to do is embrace the principles laid out in our Constitution.

Conclusion

**THE SADDEST EPITAPH WHICH CAN BE
CARVED IN MEMORY OF A VANISHED LIBERTY IS
THAT IT WAS LOST BECAUSE ITS POSSESSORS FAILED
TO STRETCH FORTH A SAVING HAND WHILE
YET THERE WAS TIME.**
— Justice George Sutherland
Associated Press v. National Labor Relations Board (1938)[1]

I n 2006, a movie came out called *Idiocracy*. In the movie, our pop
culture had so dumbed-down the people that the world was being
run by complete idiots. I know what you're thinking and, no it wasn't
a documentary. Although, sometimes I wonder if the folks in Washington
D.C. have been using it as a "how to" guide.

In the movie, everyone was using a Gatorade-style sports drink on
their crops instead of water. As you know, plants don't particularly like
sports drinks - so they weren't growing. With the country facing a food
shortage, the characters in the movie desperately tried everything they
could think of to get the crops to grow. Everything, that is, except putting
water on the crops. (Yep, it's a pretty intellectual movie.)

In the end, the main character finally convinced the people to at least
try putting water on their crops and - miracle of miracles - they started to
grow. The lesson here is, whenever you try to fight nature you're going
to struggle. Those people could have tried anything they wanted. Until
they put water on the crops they weren't going to grow - that's just how
the world works.

The same thing is true in government. We cannot continue to fight
nature and expect to be free or prosperous. If we run our government
as if all men are not created equal - or as if their individual rights are not
sacred and inalienable - we will always struggle. Our politicians can come
up with all the 10 Point Plans and Blue Ribbon Commissions they want.
Unless those plans are consistent with Natural Law, they won't be any
more effective than pouring sports drink on plants.

Fortunately, we can easily learn the Natural Laws affecting government by observing the world around us and applying a little common

[1] http://www.law.cornell.edu/supremecourt/text/301/103!

sense. That process is what you've seen throughout this book. As you look through each of the principles, notice that to reject any of them, you will have to argue that all men are not created equal. To review, here's how the logic works step by step:

1. We know that all men are created equal
2. If all men are created equal, then that tells us that:
   a. they must have rights
   b. any legitimate government must have the consent of the people being governed (because no one is born superior to the rest of us with a natural claim to rule everyone else)
3. If a government must have the consent of the people, then that tells us that:
   c. the purpose of government is to protect our rights (because no one would knowingly consent to a government whose purpose was to violate his rights)
   d. people create governments and grant them their power. Because people are the source of government power, we know that a government cannot have any power that individual citizens don't have.
4. If all men are created equal then, just as there are bad people in regular society who want to violate our rights, there will be bad people in government who want to violate our rights. Because of that we must place limits on our government to protect our rights from that government.

When we put all of that together it tells us that the only type of government that is consistent with Natural Law is a constitutionally limited government that is designed for the purpose of protecting everyone's rights equally.

You might notice that those ideas are very similar to what Thomas Jefferson wrote in the Declaration of Independence:

> "We hold these truths to be self-evident, that all men are created equal, that they are endowed by their Creator with certain inalienable rights, that among these are Life, Liberty and the pursuit of Happiness. — That to secure these rights, Governments are instituted among Men, deriving their just power from the consent of the governed..."

These are the ideas that our nation was founded on and they are all based on Natural Law. That is why the United States has been so successful.

Unfortunately, over the last few decades we've almost completely rejected these ideas. It's no coincidence that during the same time period we have also seen a steady decline in our freedom and in our stability as a nation. If we want to reverse this trend - and save the greatest nation in history - we have to start respecting Natural Law again.

We can make that happen but citizens like you and I must take the job of interpreting our Constitution back from the experts. That's our only option because they will never interpret it in a way that limits the government and protects your freedom - that's not in their best interests. The experts get their power and their wealth from making you dependent on a complicated, ever-growing government. Why in the world would they voluntarily admit that the Constitution limits their power?

We don't need to sit back helplessly and wait for the experts to tell us what the Constitution means. As you've seen throughout this book the ideas our Constitution was based on aren't rocket science - they're common sense. We are more than capable of figuring it out for ourselves and it's long past time for us to start doing exactly that.

Life is far too precious for you to allow a distant group of experts to decide how much freedom you should have. If you want to live the life you deserve, you have to take responsibility for your liberty into your own hands. It's either that, or you'll be forced to settle for the standard of living that our politicians are willing to give you. When you live at the mercy of another person like that you aren't truly living - you are just existing.

There is still time to preserve our freedom. What are you going to do to save it?

You are worth so much more than that! You only get one shot in this world - do you want to squander it by just existing? Or do you want to take control of your life and experience all that it has to offer?

You deserve to live a life where you're allowed to stand on your own two feet and see what you're made of without the politicians constantly getting in the way. A life where you can be your own man. Or your own woman. You deserve a life where you can think for yourself, where you can act for yourself, and where your life can be anything that you choose to make it.

What could be more fulfilling than that?!

www.ingramcontent.com/pod-product-compliance
Lightning Source LLC
Chambersburg PA
CBHW070813280326
41934CB00012B/3174